ISBN-13:

151 N BEACH RD, #D9
DANIA BEACH, FL 33004
12RainbowGates@gmail.com

Limits of Liability and Disclaimer of Warranty

The author and publisher shall not be liable for our misuse of this material. This book is strictly for informational, entertainment and educational purposes.. The author and/or publisher do not guarantee that anyone following these techniques, suggestions, tips, ideas, or strategies will become successful. The author and/or publisher shall have neither liability nor responsibility to anyone with respect to any loss or damage caused, or alleged to be caused, directly or indirectly by the information contained in this book.

Warnings – Disclaimers

The Twelve Steps of Alcoholics Anonymous are reprinted and adapted with permission of Alcoholics Anonymous World Services, Inc. ("AAWS") Permission to adapt the Twelve Steps does not mean that AAWS has reviewed or approved the contents of this publication, or that AAWS necessarily agrees with the views expressed herein. A.A. is a program of recovery from alcoholism only - use of the Twelve Steps in connection with programs and activities which are patterned after A.A., but which address other problems, or in any other non-A.A. context, does not imply otherwise.

The author has made every attempt to stay within the fair use of the many resources utilized in this project. Section 107 of copyright fair use law contains a list of the various purposes for which the reproduction of a particular work may be considered fair, such as criticism, comment, news reporting, teaching, scholarship, and research. Copyright protects the particular way authors have expressed themselves. It does not extend to any ideas, systems, or factual information conveyed in a work.

REALIZING EMERALD CITY: FINDING YOUR TRUE POWER ON THE YELLOW BRICK ROAD

Dedicated to the person who has been the main instrument of my True Power. My soul mate, beloved and husband-

Jagger Anand

My strength, my best fan and my "entertainer." To him, I owe my very life.

But that's another story.

Joy is a net of love by which we can catch souls.
– Mother Teresa

Contents

Acknowledgements

Thanks to all of the anonymous people who taught me how to live and love. There are simply too many to thank here since the list would count in the hundreds. But I especially think of those in Asheville, North Carolina. Some of these are my close friends. It is to them and their lives that I attribute the vision for this book.

Thank you to Donna Kozik for showing me how to put this book down on paper and to Vicky Anderson for her patience in editing it, although I admittedly kept obsessively editing even afterwards.

I also acknowledge another instrument of my True Power and my spiritual advisor, Dr. Dot. While working with her I experienced profound spiritual revelations, which lifted me to a whole new level of experience and freed me from great suffering. It was the impetus to write Realizing Emerald City.

To all the great teachers who have influenced my thinking and my Path, including: Over-Eaters Anonymous, Alcoholics Anonymous, Narcotics Anonymous, CoDa, ACOA, Judy Petrella, Chauncey Monroe Barrymore, J.J. Knodel, Bashar, Shakti Gawain, Louise Hay, Abraham-Hicks, A Course in Miracles (Jesus), Don Tritt, Ginger Tritt, Isaac Tritt, Tara Meadows, Magenta Pixie, Stephen Hawking, Masuro Emoto, Baba RamDev, Swami Jnaneshvara Bharati, Jasmuheen, Dr. Omanandji, Gurudev Amrit Desai, and so many others.

Most of all, I thank my True Power for the gift of the Slippers.

~~~~~~

God doesn't always give you what you ask for--not because you don't deserve it, but because you deserve better! --Unknown

~~~~~~

What Do We Really Want?

Most people who are dealing and living with mundane matters are generally satisfied with life. They are content with the house and the car, the job and the boss, the kids, the spouse and the dog. They might believe in God and go to church every Sunday. But they feel no need to pursue the depths of spirituality. However, people who have substance or behavioral addictions often say that they need something more.

This *more* of which these people are speaking is the calling of "the void." This is not the kind of void that Buddhists talk about, but rather it is a very empty feeling that begs to be filled no matter what the consequences. It calls for more than mere contentment with mundane pleasures. Family, pets, good food, working for a living, caring for children and so on, are just not enough. Their soul senses that there must be more than that. Have you ever said, "Is this all there is?"

Initially some will try to fill this void with different behaviors or substances. The 12 Steps of the *Alcoholics Anonymous* (AA) and *Narcotics Anonymous* (NA) recovery programs were developed because people with addictive personalities do in fact become addicted to behaviors and substances. However, even after they have entered into one of these recovery programs, the void inside them still remains. Why is that? Filling that void calls for self-actualization.

The original 12 Steps of AA are used to help people recover from alcoholism or another type of addiction. But when those same people get beyond their addictions, what they encounter are life problems. More specifically, that means the usual iving problems that most spiritually oriented people have.

Eventually, everyone who works through a recovery program must find their way to a continuous state of joy and gratitude. Unfortunately, this usually takes an extended amount of time, and averages far more than a decade in recovery. While someone is attending a recovery program, they might spend years languishing in a joyless, lackluster mentality. Of course, everyone's recovery varies and it generally improves with time. Like it states in the AA literature, "Sometimes quickly, sometimes slowly."[1]

My own personal experience, strength and hope proclaim that there is no reason to wait this long. If you do or do *not* have an addictive personality but you feel called to find a deeper meaning for your life, take a look at the program described in this book.

This book explores common philosophies from the AA program as well as from the philosophy of the laws of

---

[1] © *Alcoholics Anonymous,* Fourth Edition, page 84, reprinted with permission of Alcoholics Anonymous World Services, Inc.

attraction and *A Course in Miracles* (ACIM). It then combines them with spiritual philosophies of all the major ideologies I have found useful, into a workable system called the 12 Rainbow Gates. The 12 Rainbow Gates will form a great foundation upon which we can build our spirituality and move our life forward -- in quantum leaps.

Although the 12 Steps are focused on recovery from some type of addiction, the 12 Rainbow Gates that are described in this book promote a direct focus on a deepening spiritual awareness and quality of life. This is recovery from addiction to the 3rd dimension, anything that interferes with realization of our Self. So whether we have attended a 12 Steps program or not, we will find that by going through these 12 Rainbow Gates, our spiritual frontiers will open wide.

Indeed by working through the Rainbow Gates program that is described in this book, we will be purified mentally, emotionally and spiritually. We will be relieved of past trauma, guilt and shame. We will be less codependent and more interdependent. We will understand where we are powerless and where our power truly lies.

By working through the 12 Rainbow Gates program, we will find that spiritual practices that didn't work for us in the past will work for us now. Doors that were previously shut will open with ease. Affirmations will become powerful, miracles will occur regularly and life will begin to "flow." People will suddenly start to acknowledge our talents and abilities. They will begin to ask, "How did you do that?" We will learn about effortless effort to achieve what we need and desire. Essentially, we can be a powerhouse.

Other important spiritual lessons that are addressed in this program are effective uses of the Universal Laws of Attraction. These Universal laws *guarantee* that our entire life reflects our inner state of being. The relationship we are having is with our Self. For instance if we are feeling inner emotional chaos, we will experience increased personal chaos in our outer world, such as money and relationship problems. Times when the cable gets disconnected, the children become unbearable and the dog urinates on the floor will increase. Basically things will not go well outwardly or inwardly.

I live in a town in which there are many people who are "in recovery." Many recovering anonymous people who live here have been "clean and abstinent" for 10 to 20 years and more. That means that they are not using illicit mind or mood altering drugs or alcohol. They are living joyfully and abundantly. This is a very unique situation which I have been fortunate to observe.

Recovering people frequently say that, as their recovery progresses, they actually become *more* sensitive to pain. They are keenly aware of pain because they do not live in suffering. Whenever pain arises, they quickly make the changes that are necessary to remedy it. They would tell us that pain is an indication that something needs to be corrected. But they will also tell us that suffering is a choice.

What does that mean? No matter whether it is physical or emotional in nature, pain is a signal that something needs attention. It is an indication that something needs to change. If pain is not addressed properly, it will continue. That is suffering. The longer we stay in a state of pain, the more pain we create in our life. It becomes a vicious cycle. Pain becomes suffering and, although that suffering might appear to be caused by changing life circumstances, the chaos comes from the exact same source -- our self.

Happiness and the time that is spent in recovery are associated with one another in a positive way, increasing more or less in tandem. The more time and effort one puts into the recovery, the happier one tends to be. The word *sober* has nothing to do with being *somber*. As it says in the Alcoholics Anonymous book, titled *The Big Book*, "We are not a glum lot."[2]

Here's a scenario that I've witnessed many times: a group of professionals, primarily middle-aged, sitting in a crowded restaurant and getting louder and louder by

---

[2] © *Alcoholics Anonymous*, Fourth Edition, page 132, reprinted with permission of Alcoholics Anonymous World Services, Inc.

the minute. One wonderful, well-respected professional lady usually laughs so hard that her face turns red and the sides of her nose turn white as she tries to catch her breath. Acting as the conscientious professional, I usually mentally prepare to use the Heimlich maneuver on her. The whole group laughs and jokes, sometimes so wildly that the other people in the restaurant wonder if everyone in the group is drunk. That's the irony.

If we're reading this book, it is likely that we have already overcome tremendous obstacles in our life. We might be considered quite successful in our profession. Perhaps we are driven from one goal to the next. We might even be admired. But when we stop driving our self, we begin to feel irritable or even numb. More often than not, problems overtake our ability to cope.

In truth, this is because we are unaware of the undercurrent of irritation that is flowing inside of us, that is, until someone "gets in the way" of our plans. Then we might clench our jaw tighter or snap at them, certain that we are justified in doing so. We're afraid that everything will crack apart because we've fallen behind. After all, we work very hard to keep the bills paid.

It is possible that we were taught that our feelings don't matter, or worse yet, we have literally been taught to maintain a state of unhappiness. Maybe our family penalized or chastised us when we were young and carefree. This is far more traumatizing than we might realize.

Do not diminish the significance of joy. Losing the ability to laugh or to be conscious of joy is to misplace life's greatest gift. Once gifts like this are lost, people will try to replace them with close substitutes. This can be pride, ego, material possessions, obsessive behavior, fantasy, denial, addictions, vanity, sadism (aggression, hurtfulness or thoughtlessness) or masochism (chaos, illness, martyrdom etc).

Even worse, unhappy people will often try to make sure that others are as unhappy as they are. It is also true that "desperate people do desperate things." Similarly, an unhappy person might not consciously know that they are hurting others, but there is almost no way that they cannot do so.

The next time that you are unhappy, try an experiment. Become the beholder. Watch how you treat others. See if you hold resentments toward them. Even when we feel that we contain our self fairly well, we can still ask our Self, "Am I truly being loving to others? Am I being authentic or do I have to *try* to be pleasant?"

Now let's look at the extreme opposite personality type. Maybe you can't achieve our goals. You might even feel lazy. You can't put all of the pieces of your life together to form a pretty picture. You toss and turn in bed. Sometimes, you may even take something in order to get a good night's sleep. Then when it's time to wake up, it's hard to get going, emotionally, physically, or both. You have not even opened your eyes and yet you feel the internal struggle starting.

Maybe chaos manifests for you as discord in your partnership, lack of prosperity, lack of purpose, illness, sadness or anxiety. The symptoms are unique for everyone. The truth is that the quality of your life is a mirror of your thoughts and feelings.

Some are so grateful to rise up out of a dreadful life they were living that they continue to accept less than their highest aspirations. They begin to live a "life of quiet desperation" [cite source] in response to social conditioning. "Be responsible. Get your head out of the clouds. Get a career that makes some money and forget your unrealistic dreams." Later, not surprisingly, they ask, "Is this all there is?" No. It is just time to change things. Thank goodness for change.

We are not to blame. Indeed no one is. We have done the best we can with what we had to work with. However, we are the only ones who can change it. Perhaps we have felt a calling from our youth, which still echoes in our heart. Perhaps we feel a yearning in our heart that cannot be quenched by anything else in the mundane world. Perhaps we are a Seer, Spiritualist, Shaman, Prophet, Healer, Light Bearer, Way Shower, Star Seed, Indigo or Crystal Child.

Spiritually oriented people are often left feeling unfulfilled by mundane matters, (i.e., the house and the car, the job and the boss, the kids, the spouse and the dog). They need more than what can be seen and felt. There are many highly spiritual people who can no longer meet the requirements that have been put upon them by society, and are now homeless and living on the streets.

The good news is that we don't have to be homeless to find spirituality. We can be taken care of *and* be fulfilled too. The Rainbow Gates are for us, whether we are recovering from a "regular" addiction or from addiction to the 3rd dimension.

Addiction to the 3rd dimension is anything that interferes with your Self realization or Self actualization. Obviously it includes things like substance abuse, but there are already programs for this. The Rainbow Gates journey focuses on those situations or things that people do not normally consider addictions.

Some people are starting to realize that TV, technology, work, shopping and unhealthy foods are addictions. But what about being addicted to the social system, money, status, belongings, time, socializing, gossip, medicine, compliments, respect, information, electricity, autos, fast food, etc. This list is not exhaustive by any means. The ego always wants "more." It wants more of everything.

As long as it can keep us distracted with attaining those things, we are delayed in awakening. It is nice to enjoy the road home, but there is a difference in dependency and mere enjoyment. For example, there is much difference in social drinking and alcoholism.

Anything that we are dependent on may delay our awakening and return. That is the reason the Rainbow Gates were created.

~~~~~~~~~~~~~~~~~~~~~~~~~~~~~~~~

"Nothing real can be threatened. Nothing unreal exists. Herein lies the peace of God."-ACIM[3]

~~~~~~~~~~~~~~~~~~~~~~~~~~~~~~~~

[3] ACIM = A Course in Miracles. This fabulous text is channeled by Dr. Helen Schucman. For more information got to ACIM.org

What and Where is Nowhere?

In *A Course In Miracles* (ACIM), it is stated, "Nothing real can be threatened. Nothing unreal exists. Herein lies the peace of God." So if nothing unreal exists and nothing real can be threatened, but we are feeling threatened anyway, who is threatened?

First, our ego *feels* threatened. That doesn't mean that we are threatened. It's just a feeling. I am not saying that feelings are not facts. They might be; they might not be. But, if a feeling is not of love, then it is not real. Only love is real.

If we are experiencing a feeling that is not of love, but rather is associated with fear or stems from fear, (e.g., anger, envy, jealousy, depression, etc.), we are experiencing something that is unreal. This is because nothing real can be threatened. So it is just the unreal part of us that is feeling threatened. What part of us feels threatened? Our conscious mind -- the ego -- feels threatened. We are identifying with and seeing life through the eyes of the ego, the negative aspect of our consciousness. Although the ego is not real, it can *feel* threatened. We can live its dream, its illusion.

If the ego is not real, where does the ego exist? It exists in a state of our mind that is also not real. It lives in an illusory place that is, more or less, threatening, dark, chaotic, burdensome, depressing and draining.

Since this place is not real, it is nowhere. So let's call this place of illusion the Nightmare of Nowhere.

Now we might be asking, "How can my world be unreal?" Because our five senses of sight, sound, touch, taste and smell are extremely powerful. It is more accurate to say that our *perception* is extremely powerful. We *believe* that our world is external to us. However, our perception of our external world exists in our mind.

There is plenty of scientific proof of this. Our eyes don't actually see light; our ears don't actually hear sound. Neuro-psychologists and nuclear physicists agree that our brain *interprets* visual and auditory input as light and sound waves. So it interprets and processes all of our senses. But what if those senses are also not accurately interpreting?

At birth we could not make sense of all of the visual and auditory input that we received. Visual and auditory input has no meaning to an infant. But with time, we started to assign meanings to things. Later we assigned judgment to these things as "good" or "bad." Our mother's face meant love and pleasure; the dog's bark meant danger. This assignment of meaning creates perceptions, which is how learning and conditioning occur. So now we must *unlearn* and *un-condition* our self. Another way to say this is: we must remove the blocks to the awareness of the love that surrounds us.

Many naïve people live within the Gates of Nowhere. But Nowhere is an unreal realm; it is a "state of mind." It is not reality, but it is definitely a real experience. We encourage you to do our own research on quantum physics, bio-physics and neuro-psychology. A great place to start is by viewing the short 2004 documentary, titled "*What the Bleep Do We Know*," which posits a spiritual connection between consciousness and quantum physics.

Our dreams are as *real* as our wakeful experience. They are dreams within a dream. Contrary to popular belief, an intense dream or a nightmare affects us just as profoundly as our conscious wakeful experience. Many children who live in the east are taught to master their dreams. When children awaken from a nightmare, they should not be told that what they experienced wasn't real. Just tell them they are safe now.

Many religions, from the Mayans to the Bushmen, from the Buddhists to some Christians, believe that our entire existence is just a dream. Indeed, it is a dream. Even in the Holy Bible it states that Adam went to sleep, but it does not say that he awakened from it.

Many people do not realize that they are living in the Nightmare of Nowhere. They think that they are living in reality. They don't know that there is happier place in which they could be living.

Most of the people who live in the Nightmare of Nowhere are fairly accepting of their situation and can make sense of it. They never consider leaving because it represents sanity to them. They are like a fish in water. When we point out to the fish where it lives, the fish says, "What water?" It is often the same in Nowhere. In order for us to understand insanity, we must be insane. So it's best that we don't even try.

But there are some fish that are more awake and aware. They might reply, "Oh yeah. I agree that this water could be better, but that's just how it's always been. We can't get above the water line or we'll die." These are the people who can see the edges of the Nightmare of Nowhere, but are still deeply frightened. It takes courage to escape the nightmare.

"Will it be worth it to get out of Nowhere, or will it just be more of the same? Is it real? How do I know? Will I be taken up in a beam of light? Will I just disappear? What lies on the other side? What if it is not better? Can I come back? Who will help me? What if I'm wrong? Could I lose what little I have now? Will others think I am crazy? Am I crazy?"

A few people realize that they have spent their life trying to get Somewhere while living a lie in Nowhere. They are exhausted by the chaos, lies, death, disease and destruction -- the suffering. They feel that they can no longer perform the work that is required to get out.

Furthermore, it seems impossible to get out. So they choose to give up completely, and sadly end their lives.

If you are considering taking this route, we ask that you give the Rainbow Gates a try. Since we are eternal beings, in all likelihood we will be required to complete these lessons anyway. So why not choose something different now. Remember that we are under contract to be here at this momentous time. It was no small decision to be here and no small feat to get here.

Let's talk about the flying fish. Flying fish are very aware of other possibilities from which they can choose. These types of fish know that they can live Somewhere other than in water. So they jump joyfully out of the water and into the air. They are waking up from the dream. We are waking masters and the Universe is joyfully watching every move.

We consider our self fortunate if we have realized that we can leave the Nightmare of Nowhere. If we do our research, our questions will be answered and our fears will be managed. It will not be an easy journey, but it will be worth it. Yes, the solution is real. Our life *will* be super-powered. We will experience joy, miracles and coincidences that will thrill us. We will experience love and we will feel loving.

The closer we get to reality, the happier we will be. We will be on our way Somewhere. No, we will not go up in a beam of light. Nor will we disappear, although that has happened to a few yogis who have worked very hard. We get out of anything what we put into it.

If we don't like the Happy Dream, we can always return to the Nightmare of Nowhere. As a matter of fact, most likely, we *will* return - innumerable times. We will be tempted to return when we are challenged by certain situations and events. Perhaps we will find our self feeling justified in anger and refusing to forgive a heinous deed. In that case, we will remain in the Nightmare of Nowhere for as long as it takes us to change our mind. Perhaps a death in the family triggers us to react with remorse. Basically, we will be living the nightmare until we can view death a different way.

The longer we stay in the Nightmare of Nowhere, the harder it will be to get back on the path to Somewhere. But we will always be shown the way out, no matter how many times we return. The tools will always work. Sometimes, we will simply have to chisel through a thin plaster wall. At other times, it might feel like a thick, concrete, prison wall. Frankly, it depends on how long we stay and our reasons for staying.

But that's alright. That is part of the contrast that we must experience so that we can choose where we want to reside. We always have free will.

~~~~~~~~~~~~~~~~~~~~~~~~~

There are only two mistakes one can make along the road to truth; not starting and not going all the way.

– The Buddha[4]

~~~~~~~~~~~~~~~~~~~~~~~~~

---

[4] Read more at http://www.brainyquote.com

A True but not Necessarily Factual Story

One night, an official from Nowhere noticed a seeker who was far, far out on the fringe of Nowhere. Nowhere officials are dreamers who try to keep seekers from awakening and leaving (A.k.a. Nowhere Man). It is their job to control the seekers who lurk on the edge of the nightmare and to discourage them from seeking.

The Nowhere official asks the seeker, "What are you searching for way out here on the fringes?" The seeker replies, "I'm looking for a way out. Do you know of one?" The Nowhere official scratches his head, "A way out of where?" The seeker quickly realizes that he could be stereotyped as one of those crazy people. So he quickly recants, "Oh, never mind. I've had too many drinks."

The seeker's retraction satisfies the official who then offers to give the seeker a ride home, back toward the heart of the nightmare. But the closer to they get, the more painful the ride becomes to the seeker. The interaction between the official and the awakening seeker becomes darker, heavier and more sinister by the mile. As they drive back to the dark heart of Nowhere, the more threatened, desperate and full of despair the awakening seeker begins to feel.

Before the seeker gets out of the automobile, the official gives him a referral for a program that will get him back on track to being a "good" citizen to the town of Nightmares. The seeker thanks the official and enters the dark, empty house. He throws down his coat. Then he 'throws down' some drinks to numb his 'pain.'

Dorothy, his wife and partner of five years, had a rough childhood. She was plagued by an eating disorder, and was an alcoholic and addict. At times, she could also be very naïve and irresponsible. She was the black sheep of her family. She was always searching for the meaning of life.

Dorothy and the seeker separated just one week prior. That was part of the reason why he was searching intensely at the edge of the Nightmare of Nowhere. Dorothy had been talking to him about leaving and going "home." But she was not referring to her parent's home. With great enthusiasm she described to him a place where the nightmare changes into the happy dream.

Dorothy went on to tell him that, in order to get Somewhere, which is reality, we have to pass through the happy dream. She said that, although it exists within Nowhere, the happy dream more closely reflects reality and that, the longer someone remains there, the more closely reality is reflected back to them. Eventually, they pass easily into reality, which is everyone's *true* home.

He asked Dorothy why someone can't just pass from the nightmare to the reality that awaits us. She said that, in truth, everyone is *already* at home in reality, but that we are asleep. We are simply asleep in Nowhere. When we are asleep in Nowhere, our experience can manifest as a happy dream or it can manifest as a nightmare.

It is impossible for someone to pass from a nightmare into reality because they would perceive everything in reality as frightening. So the happy dream was created to *reflect* reality so that people can practice awakening into, and then living in reality. The happy dream is a bridge or stopover from which people gently waken into reality.

It is these types of discussions that initially brought he and Dorothy together. They had sparked in each other the belief that there is something more to life. They would sit on the porch and smoke cigarettes, while they talked endlessly about topics of a spiritual nature. That was their favorite pastime.

But the talks that used to uplift and inspire them were now turning into a "mind field" (pun intended). The seeker no longer had any time for this "rubbish." Sure, he had his moments when he was young, when he explored that "hippie stuff." But he had grown up and, although he tried to remain calm, he was getting very agitated with all of the nonsense that was now taking place. What did Dorothy mean by "leaving Nowhere?" As she talked about places, such as Somewhere, Nowhere, reality and home, he could feel that he was losing her.

Unfortunately, it seemed that what she was looking for was not to be found in their life together, but rather, in their lives apart. He acknowledged that life appeared to be more difficult for his wife than it was for him. So they mutually agreed to a separation. Then he read a book about how to "let go."

He decided that this was just a postpartum stage of Dorothy's life and that, as long as he didn't make an issue of it, she would soon get over it. Eventually, she would come to the conclusion that living here and now isn't so bad after all. If it was good enough for Ram Dass, surely it is good enough for her.

But the look in her eyes was so far off that, sometimes, it seemed as though she was coming unglued. He recognized this look in the eyes of other people too. Usually it was when they were under the influence of drugs, such as LSD or marijuana, or when they were talking about another dimension of reality. That's it, he thought. She must be abusing drugs again. Or, perhaps, what her family implied was true – that she's "light on the top end."

Dorothy continued to be dissatisfied, lethargic and depressed. As time went on, the condition of their house began to reflect her growing detachment. The house was not decorated, despite the fact that she was an artist. Very few pictures hung on the wall. Cooking did not give her enjoyment. Her heart was empty, so their food was not prepared with love.

One day, she asked him, "I am planning on going through the Rainbow Gates. Would you go with me?" "No," he ardently told her. He had decided that she was crazy and was abusing drugs. Now he was secretly preparing for her departure and had retained an attorney.

Before she finally "disappeared," Dorothy asked him several more times if he would join her. But each time, he declined. So, despite her fears, she had no choice but to heed her calling and move forward.

Eventually, Dorothy went on to tell stories about her great journeys and the true love she found beyond the Rainbow Gates. However, she only told her stories to those who yearned for something more.

~~~~~~~~~~~~~~~~~~~~~~~~~~~~~~~~

I've always taken 'The Wizard of Oz' very seriously, you know. I believe in the idea of the rainbow. And I've spent my entire life trying to get over it.

-Judy Garland[5]

~~~~~~~~~~~~~~~~~~~~~~~~~~~~~~~~

---

[5] Read more at http://www.brainyquote.com

The Allegory of Oz

An allegory is a representation of abstract ideas that are interpreted in such a way as to reveal a hidden meaning. This particular allegory is about the journey home to reality, which Dorothy talked about. It is a search for knowledge, heart and courage – a search through the 12 Rainbow Gates.

Many of us are already familiar with the story of the Wizard of Oz. The theatrical production is timeless. At the beginning of that movie, there is a dedication to those people who are young at heart and who recognize its timeless philosophy. But what is *most* interesting is that the creators of the movie embedded hidden meaning into the story.

The Wizard of Oz story, as it is best known, was a grand feat to reveal esoteric knowledge. This knowledge could not be spoken of directly to most of the audiences that are living in Nowhere because it would have provoked their ego. But, by embedding lessons deeply into the story, the ego is not affected or insulted when the story is told. Aren't many great lessons told in parable for this very reason? So let us begin by establishing the meaning of the symbols in the story...

The state of Kansas represents "Home," but not the home that we grew up in. Kansas represents reality, which is our *true* home. Some might view this as Heaven or Nirvana.

In contrast, the land of Oz represents Nowhere - our illusory state of mind. The tornado that lifts up the farmhouse from Kansas, and then sets it down in the land of Oz, represents a deep disturbance in Dorothy's mind and therefore in reality. However, in truth, there can be no disturbance in reality, so this is an illusion in itself.

The farmhouse is symbolic of the dreaming state of our minds.   It represents both the "negative" and "positive" attributes of our personality – our ego.

The Emerald City represents the state of mind in which we are *preparing* to go home to reality. It is the happy dream of Oz. All of life is an illusion. But, in the illusion of Emerald City, we can live a life in which we *feel* joyful. Our feelings actually emit signals, or energetic "vibrational frequencies." The higher vibrational frequencies energize us; the lower vibrational frequencies drain us.

Science is now starting to prove this phenomenon. One theory is that there is an energy field that extends 15 feet out from our heart. The heart is a highly energetic organ. When we get hurt, this can create a great amount of strain on the heart. The heart reacts to everything we experience – both "positively" and "negatively."

The Emerald City is the place in which we can raise our vibrational frequencies higher and higher until we are emitting pure vibrant frequencies. Then, when we are ready, we can ascend back to our *true* home, just like Dorothy does in Oz.

The little dog, Toto, represents our emotional attachments, such as children or other loved ones whom we feel compelled to protect. We can have many other material attachments too, like our home, food or work.

Glinda is the "good" witch. She can be viewed as God, Spirit, Source, the Divine, the Creator, Mother, the Great Companion, our Super-Consciousness, our Higher Self, our Higher Power or our True Power. For the purposes of this book, I will use the term *True Power* because, as we progress spiritually, we begin to realize that this Power actually works with us to co-create our lives. This is not an egotistical position but, rather, it is just a perspective. As a co-creator with our True Power, we accept responsibility for our own perceptions within the illusion.

Our True Power exists outside of both time and space. It exists outside of the illusion. So it can literally see the bigger picture of our life. We can consider our True Power as the Super-Consciousness about which Sigmund Freud and Carl Jung have both written. There is really nothing mystical about this element of the personality. It is well documented in the psychology community.

The 12 Rainbow Gates will hopefully open the concept of a True Power. Any rationalist, agnostic or atheist can take comfort in this idea. Our True Power holds our highest ideals and principles, and is far more intelligent than our conscious mind, or ego. Indeed, unlike our ego, our True Power (Super Consciousness, etc.) is unlimited in its power and knowledge.

If we examine the story of Oz, Dorothy's journey begins in Munchkin land. Munchkin land is a fabulous place. The residents *seem* to be happy. But it is frequently terrorized by the wicked witch of the west – the "bad" witch. In contrast to our True Power, the wicked witch represents our darkest ego. She represents our lower vibrational frequencies - our lower self. The witch represents anything that stands in the way of love, truth and joy. It is interesting to note that, in the story of Oz, the witch is also represented by the character, Alvira Gulch, who appears at the beginning of the story.

The wicked witch of the west presents challenges to Dorothy that she must overcome. Everything and everyone is just a reflection of our self... There is no one else.

One successful psychologist explains self-centered ego-driven people this way, *"Look at how much pain this other person is in. They are pitiful. Thank goodness I am not like that."* But in fact, they are like that in some way.

They are simply detached from their own pain because they are projecting it onto someone else.

The deepest and darkest parts of Oz are the forests, particularly where the wicked witch lives. The forests in Oz represent the darkest and most confusing parts of our lives. The dark forest is symbolic of how we perceive places, things and situations; the witch symbolizes how we see our self or therefore others. Let us thank her for her gift of awareness.

People who live in the forests of Oz have been deeply hurt. They have often lost the ability to deal with their feelings directly. So they have shut them down. When we shut down our feeling centers, we actually shut down the *ability* to feel. We cannot feel pain, nor can we feel happiness, joy and love. This is a sad situation that calls for love.

If we are in a relationship with a negative person, we can expect to experience physical or emotional problems. But don't blame them. They probably cannot change at this time. Try to remember that it is our decision to stay with them so we can learn whatever life lesson we need to learn, even if that lesson is simply to learn when to walk away-peacefully.

Such people reside deep in the dark forest of Oz, helping to solidify the desires of others to awaken and to get out of Oz. That's their job. They are our greatest teachers. Accept them, forgive them, thank them and pray for a miracle.

Of course, we can be *called* back into the dark forest of Oz at any time. This happens to Dorothy, the tin woodsman, the scarecrow and the lion. But that's how we learn the life lessons that we need to learn in order to live in reality. It is our choice if we want to return to Oz after we learn all of our life lessons. But ideally, we will spend less and less time in the dark forests of Oz and become semi-permanent residents of the Emerald City, before returning home to reality.

At the beginning of the Oz story, there is trouble in Kansas. Alvira Gulch (the wicked witch of the west) has threatened to have Toto destroyed because he supposedly bit her. The idea of being separated from her little dog is too much for Dorothy's mind. Separation and the idea of separation do not exist in reality.

For Dorothy, this is this idea that manifests the illusion of separation. It is enough to immediately disrupt her perception of Home, create the illusion of the land of Oz and all its illusory characters. By her belief that separation is a possibility, her dream begins. She falls deeper into the illusion even as she comes up with her own solutions to that illusion. Problems cannot be solved from the same level that created them.

Dorothy begins to dream of a place in which there are no problems – a place that is somewhere over the rainbow. Shortly thereafter, Alvira comes to take Toto away. She leaves with him in a basket. Luckily, Toto escapes from Alvira and runs back to Dorothy. Dorothy then runs away from home and asks Professor Marvel to take her and Toto with him to see new places.

Professor Marvel convinces Dorothy to return home because her Aunt Em misses her terribly. As Dorothy begins to run back to her Aunt Em, the tornado suddenly pops up in Kansas. Unfortunately, her family have already entered the storm cellar and have locked it behind them. Symbolically, Dorothy is now locked out of Heaven. She is *torn* from her beloveds. The idea of separation is the basis for the 'grand illusion.'

When Dorothy cannot gain access to the storm cellar, she takes shelter in her bedroom in the farmhouse. There, an object hits her on the head and she falls unconscious. When she awakens, she realizes that she is no longer home in Kansas. She is in a very strange place called Oz. She says, "We're not in Kansas anymore, Toto."

At first, the land of Oz is delightful. It is full of amazing creatures and interesting people. Isn't this like our lives when we are very young? The world seems so amazing and rich, and so full of possibilities. Particularly as children, an intense dream or a nightmare affects us just as profoundly as a conscious wakeful experience.

The Land of Oz *seems* real to Dorothy. But she is in an unreal, illusory place.

Glinda, the good witch, welcomes Dorothy to Oz. But Dorothy has already decided that she wants to return home. Dorothy has recognized that she is in a place in which she does not belong. It is at this point in the story where she passed through the 1st Rainbow Gate. This is the Gate of Illusion.

The Munchkins in Munchkin land proclaim Dorothy their national heroine because, as Glinda points out, when Dorothy's house landed in Oz, it landed on the wicked witch of the east and killed her. This liberated the Munchkins. So Glinda sings a song to them:

> come out, come out
> wherever you are
> and meet the young lady
> who fell from a star
> she fell from the sky
> she fell very far

When Dorothy tells Glinda that she wants to go home, Glinda gives her the ruby slippers that belonged to the dead witch. She tells Dorothy that they will take her home.

At this point in the story, things change dramatically when the wicked witch of the west appears and accuses Dorothy of killing her sister, the wicked witch of the east. The fact that Dorothy is wearing the ruby slippers angers the wicked witch of the west even more. The shoes hold power that the witch feels only she deserves. Glinda warns Dorothy never to take off the ruby slippers - "Keep tight inside of them. There magic must be very powerful..." The slippers hold a mystical power that will ultimately get Dorothy home – to her true reality.

It is interesting to note that the color of the witch's skin is green. Could it be that she is green with envy? Like the witch, the darker side of the ego desires power, but it cannot rightly use, share or *appreciate* power. The negative aspects of the ego never have enough money, prestige or acknowledgment. The ego is part of the illusion. So we cannot take the ego 'home' with us. The positive aspects of the ego can enter the Emerald City and have a function. But the ego will always stay in the land of Oz.

When the witch threatens Dorothy, Glinda simply laughs. She says, "Be gone. You have no power here." Glinda carries such a high vibrational frequency she is not threatened by the witch.

The witch then disappears in a flurry of red smoke and flames. Glinda exclaims, "Oh, what a smell of sulfur." This is an old reference to evil and to Satan, or the devil. So, it is safe to assume that the wicked witch represents any meaningful form of resistance to good in our lives.

At this point, Dorothy lets Glinda know that she would give anything to get out of the Land of Oz. Dorothy trusts Glinda. This is the 2nd Rainbow Gate that requires trust in a True Power.

Glinda advises Dorothy to ask the wizard of Oz to take her home. She and the Munchkins send Dorothy down the yellow brick road toward the Emerald City. The moment before Dorothy takes her first step onto the yellow brick road, she moves through the 3rd Rainbow Gate – the Gate of Decision. It is a decision to cooperate with Glinda's guidance. Dorothy decided to complete the journey Glinda laid before her to follow the yellow brick road.

Later, some distance down the road, Dorothy meets the scarecrow. Take note that he is mounted at a crossroad. He tells Dorothy that either direction is a good way to go. Symbolically, this means there are many roads that lead home to reality. They are all good. We just need to pick one.

As Dorothy longs to go home - the scarecrow desires a brain. He believes that, if he has a brain, he can acquire knowledge. If he has knowledge, others will respect him, especially the crows that keep picking at him. This is symbolic of the 4th Rainbow Gate- the Gate of Knowledge.

In the 4th Gate, we attain self-knowledge. It is appropriate that the scarecrow is encountered at the beginning of this Gate because self-knowledge is the most important kind of knowledge, is it not? As Socrates said, "a life unexamined is not worth living." Paradoxically, though the scarecrow thinks he lacks brains, he is the one that comes up with great plans.

Soon, Dorothy and the scarecrow encounter the tin woodsman. His rusted state is akin to rigidity and frozenness. The tin woodsman claims that, when the tinsmith created him, he forgot to give him a heart. It is a great analogy because, when people forget to love and enjoy life, they become hollow, rigid and rusty. The tin man sings:

If I only had a heart
I'd be tender and sentimental
Regarding love and art
I'd be friends with the sparrows
And the boys who shoot the arrows
If I only had a heart...

The tin woodsman joins Dorothy and the scarecrow on their journey. Ironically, he cries more than anyone else in the story. Why? He already has a heart. He just has a *sad* heart.

Dorothy feels like she has known the tin man and the scarecrow for a long time. Maybe it is because they are reflections of some part of her? We have arrived at the 5th Rainbow Gate – the Gate of Humbleness. In this Gate, there is the sharing of a personal story with select comrades. There's a feeling of connection, transparency and shared journey as they reveal intimate perceptions of themselves. We might even call them soul mates. Dorothy longs to go home, the scarecrow desires a brain and the tin woodsman wants a heart.

The 6th Rainbow Gate is the Gate of Willingness. At this Gate, the witch appears and tells the scarecrow and the tin man to abandon Dorothy. But the witch's threats only strengthen their resolve to continue their journey. They demonstrate their willingness to reach their destination, despite all the odds. Symbolically, each time the members of the group re-affirm their goals of attaining what they desire, (i.e., a home, knowledge, a heart), they pass through the 6th Gate.

Each time the group desire and envision themselves receiving the gifts, which they believe they will receive from the wizard, they are practicing the 7th Rainbow Gate – the Gate of Purification. The first part of this Gate pertains to the process of 'asking.' In this Gate, we ask for the removal of the blocks to the awareness of the love that surrounds us, or for the removal of those character traits that no longer serve us.

If the group thought that the wizard could hear them as they traveled along the yellow brick road, they would have simply asked him right where they stood. But, by following the yellow brick road they are in the *process* of asking, since their primary purpose in reaching Emerald City is to ask the wizard for help. Beyond willingness, action demonstrates decision and sincerity of purpose. This is a good parallel since the 7th Gate is often more of a process than an event. However, there are commonly immediate and miraculous gifts within this Gate.

The purpose of the 7th Gate is to receive gifts from our True Power. All of the characters in the Oz story seem to be exceptionally adept at visualizing how they will *feel* after they have received their gifts from the wizard. They even sing songs about it. Dorothy is being assisted by gifts of knowledge and heart (in the form of the scarecrow and the tin man) despite the fact no one seems to realize at this point in the journey.

A Course in Miracles speaks about removing the blocks to the awareness of love that surrounds us. Essentially, this means that love is all around us but, if we have blocks to the *awareness* of it, we will not *realize* it. We already have everything; we already are everything. Love is everything. The Oz group is not seeking to have something removed; each of them is seeking to *receive* something - or realize something. This is simply a matter of perception. In other words, a 'defect' is a block to the awareness of love - and all its expressions. To realize that the gifts they are seeking are already within them they must continue on the yellow brick road.

Nothing can be added to us. That is the conundrum. So a grand illusion has been created. Oz is an illusion. The lie is that we are imperfect, we are lost and that we are not home. In its diverse forms, what we are asking to have removed is the illusion itself. Perfect love has always existed; we have always been perfect love.

Now back to Oz... Together the three friends travel deeper into the dark forest. The scarecrow stammers, "Of course, I don't know but I think it'll get darker before it gets lighter." Indeed, this is often the case. When things change for the better, they often initially appear to be worse. The illusion of darker darkness can be temporarily part of the journey.

This is the point in the story at which the three friends meet the lion. The lion represents both fear and the desire for its removal. Courage is necessary at this point in the journey. Courage is not fearlessness but enables us to act *despite* our fear. Courage is needed to keep facing deeper layers of our false self, which is what is required to complete the journey. Fearlessness is the ultimate reward for courageousness given that facing our fears gives us opportunity to master them. The 8th and 9th Gates are excellent preparation for fearlessness.

In the dark forest the lion jumps out from the behind a tree. He tries to intimidate the whole group, including Toto, the little dog. The lion chases Toto around a tree and tries to bite him. Dorothy slaps the lion's face in an effort to stop his attack. This snaps him out of his arrogant façade and he begins to cry. He confesses that he is actually a *cowardly* lion. He makes amends to the whole group. This is the 9th Gate – the Gate of Love. He expresses regret and a desire to change. He does not defend his behavior. This is done in the true spirit of amending a relationship.

The moments before the lions confessed; when he knew he was 'in the wrong,' was the 8th Gate. This is the gate of Thoughtfulness. Usually, we want to take time with thoughtfulness. We want to think (be thoughtful) about what we are going to say and how we are going to say it. But, in the lion's defense it was an awkward moment.

When Dorothy slapped the lion's face, it was in defense of Toto. So she did not need to apologize for her actions nor did she. Nor did the group have to accept the lion's apology. But they did. They even invited the lion along on their journey to see the wizard. Great miracles of love are often returned to us at the 9th Gate of Love and doors open for us which were previously closed. The lion, delighted, bursts into a ditty:

> Yeah, it's sad believe me missy
>
> When you're born to be a sissy
>
> Without the vim and verve
>
> But I could show my prowess
>
> Be a lion and not a mouse
>
> If I only had the nerve...

Our friends have now passed through the 8th and 9th Gates of Thoughtfulness and Love. The Oz clan can see the Emerald City. They dart toward it. Dorothy longs to go home, the scarecrow desires a brain, the tin woodsman wants a heart and the cowardly lion is wishing that he had courage. They are feeling victorious. They believe the long journey is nearly over and they are overcome with excitement.

Unfortunately, the wicked witch has been watching our friends through her crystal ball. She manifests poisoned poppies all across the yellow brick road almost completely obscuring their path. The poppies are fragrant and attractive to the eye. They are tempting distractions - like all the amazing people, places and things in the material world. When distractions tempt us from our Path, we fall asleep.

The Oz group is now standing at the 10th Gate. This is the Gate of Commitment. At this point, it can be difficult to stay focused on the journey because lack of ongoing commitment. We could simply fall back asleep. The 10th Gate is the first of three Rainbow Gates which ensure that we keep our hard won freedom and consciousness.

Dorothy, Toto and the lion fall into a deep sleep but the tin man and the scarecrow start yelling, "Help. Help." Thank goodness for travelling companions - right? Glinda hears their cries causing it to snow. This, in turn, awakens Dorothy, Toto and the lion.

It is noteworthy that Glinda is able to answer their pleas at this point. The group has done their legwork and they simply called out for a miracle – and they got it. They can now access power that previously eluded them. The group called out for help and the power to complete their mission. This is the first part of the 11th Gate – seeking conscious contact through prayer (or yelling for help as necessary). As they finish their crossing through the poppies toward the Emerald City angelic voices can be heard from the sky.

You're out of the woods
You're out of the dark
You're out of the night
Step into the sun
Step into the light
Keep sending it forth
For the most glorious days on the earth...

The angelic serenade represents the end of the journey through the dark forest. The group has literally made it out of the woods. They realize that they have completed a lot of hard work that is now paying off. Inspired, they skip joyfully down the yellow brick road, toward the Emerald City. They are awakened to a vision more beautiful than their dreams. How splendid is that vision of Emerald City. They can now enjoy ever widening dimensions of awareness and truth within – if they are allowed to enter its gates.

At the Gate to the Emerald City, they ring a bell that hangs on the door. This irritates the Gatekeeper. He asks them why they didn't read the instructions that are attached to the door. Our friends tell him that there is nothing on the door for them to read. So he attaches instructions to the door. The instructions state that visitors to the Emerald City must knock to gain entrance to the city – not ring the bell.

This is a somewhat significant lesson regarding the unwritten rules of spirituality. We begin our journey by doing what we know how to do and we won't be perfect at it. We find out what works as we grope along.

The Gatekeeper of Emerald City only lets our friends enter the Gate only when he sees that Dorothy is wearing the ruby slippers. Is this because only those people who have certain magical powers or disciplines can make contact with their True Power? No - The ruby slippers were given to Dorothy *after* she asked for Glinda's help. She began to trust Glinda at the 2nd Gate, before she started on her journey to Emerald City.

At this point in the story, the group is taken away so they can "be prepared" to meet the wizard. This represents the purification that is sought when we pass through the 7th Gate. Often, most of the results of our hard work show up at this stage of our journey. In the Oz story, Dorothy gets a new dress; the scarecrow gets new stuffing; the tin man has rust removed; the lion is pampered.

Basically, to the extent that we prepare our self for a relationship with our True Power, we can enter the inner chambers within it. That is the main purpose of the previous Gates. When we trust and cooperate with our True Power and reasonably purify our minds we can enter the inner sanctum.

The group truly feels that they are on their way to their happy dream. Indeed, they are experiencing happy dreams. Without warning, the witch flies above the Emerald City and writes "SURRENDER DOROTHY" in the sky with her scraggly broom. What does this mean?

Symbolically, Dorothy's expanding consciousness is uncovering the dark root of the ego. This happens when we start 'clearing' lower vibrational frequencies. Unpleasant things will unexpectedly pop up and trigger a reaction. This takes place so that we can resolve and release them. We surrender- but not to the darkness. We just accept what is right now. We ceased fighting. We can't fight; at least not directly. We ask for help and listen for guidance. This is how we heal and as we heal our self we heal others.

In this process, we will start to affect others around us. We may find that, when we start a new job or join a group, chaos abounds, despite our best intentions to blend with others. Hidden truths are uncovered and we end up seeing the pink elephant that no one else seems to notice. Any reaction that is not of love is of fear. Do not fear. Fear is just a call for love; ours or someone else's. Just trust that there is a purpose. Our True Power will help us and what we are experiencing can be for the highest good of everyone concerned.

In the Oz story, Dorothy has *drawn* the witch to the Emerald City but the witch cannot enter. The Oz clan runs to their guru for help - the wizard of Oz. But the wizard has his own agenda. Before he will give our friends everything that they want, he demands that they bring the witch's broom to him. Although this is far from selfless on the wizard's part; good still comes from this. Nothing goes to waste in God's economy, particularly when there is spirit of service. This is the 12th Gate - the Gate of Service.

When we go through this 12th Gate, we might find that we are drawn back into the illusion for some reason, but from a higher perspective. This may be of our own volition, or as a result of someone else's request, or in order to help others.

Sometimes our undesired character traits draw us back into the dark forest. This need not harm us. Instead, if we listen closely to our True Power, we will be able to make significant gains. Others will too. Miracles will happen. According to *A Course in Miracles*, miracles are a way of giving to those who temporarily have less by those who temporarily have more. We cannot keep what we have unless we give it away. We have to give it away to realize it.

Let's return to Oz... The group finds themselves back in the dark forest, heading toward the castle of the wicked witch. She sends her monkey minions to seize Dorothy and Toto, leaving the others stranded in the forest.

Back at the castle, the witch tries to convince Dorothy to give her the ruby slippers. Dorothy concedes when the witch threatens to drown Toto. As always, Toto escapes and leads the rest of the group back to the castle. They attempt to rescue Dorothy, but are cornered by the witch and her soldiers.

When the witch lights the scarecrow on fire, Dorothy puts out the fire by throwing water on him. The water splashes up onto the witch. In this case, water represents Spirit dissolving the negative parts of the ego. Because the witch represents the antithesis of Spirit, the water neutralizes her. The witch cries as she melts away:

What a world
What a world
Who would have thought
A good girl like you
Could destroy my wonderful wickedness

"Ding. Dong. The Wicked Witch is dead. By killing the witch, Dorothy not only liberates herself, but everyone else in Oz, as well. How fabulous is that. The witch's minions are grateful that the witch is dead because they are now liberated.

In dissolving the witch, Dorothy resolved some of the darkness within herself (her own shadow self). It takes darkness to know darkness. 'Dissolving' is symbolism for the dissolution of undesired characteristics. Indeed, often it is a process of dissolution. Always practice acceptance, patience along our path. It's about progress not perfection.

The uprooting of darkness from our life will be a path unique to us. Our life lessons all stem from the release of fear. In other words, miracles are the removal of blockages to the awareness of the love that surrounds us and of the love that *is* us.

Dorothy takes the witch's broom back to the wizard. But the entire group is bewildered when the wizard tells them to come back the next day. When Toto pulls back the veil that conceals the man behind the curtain, everyone realizes that he really isn't the wizard he proclaims himself to be.

There is so much hidden meaning that is implied in this part of the story. This type of disappointment occurs when we realize that religion, gurus, teachers and other role models do not have all of the answers. They are far from the ideals we unfairly placed on them. We may even realize that, if they did it, so can we. This is actually a stage of development at which people start to look inward for their own answers and guidance. This is the way it is supposed to work.

When the group becomes angry with the wizard for being a fraud, they call him a "bad" man. Judging is the labeling of something as "bad" or "good" or "better" or "worse." The wizard replies, "No, I am a good man. I am just a bad wizard." He is actually fairly humble in making amends. There is no need to condemn others for being human or for being less than godly. However, we tend to be tempted to do just that. We avoid this trap. It only takes us backward.

At the beginning of the story, Glinda says that the wizard is a "good" man, but that he is very mysterious. We need to remember this lesson when we come upon our own "bad" wizards. They will be giving us a gift that will help us to realize our own power. Keep in mind that everything and everyone we encounter on our Path is exactly the way they are supposed to be. They are there for our ultimate good.

After the wizard gives his apologies to the group, he awards the scarecrow with a diploma to show him that he is *already* intelligent. He then shows the lion that it is his fear that has enabled him to survive in the woods. He also shows him that, in facing the things that have frightened him, he was actually *demonstrating* courage. The wizard gives the lion a medal of courage to show him that he had been brave all along.

Then, the wizard wonders why the tin man wants a heart, since hearts can be broken. The tin man insists that, even though this may be the case, he still wants a heart. So the wizard shows him that he *already* possesses the heart he so desires. The wizard points out that the tin man is a "do-gooder." He gives him a ticking heart pendant. If we notice, the tin man cries several times throughout the story, due to his compassionate and caring nature.

It is interesting to note that the very thing that is desired by each of our friends is already within them. The lesson here is that, if we desire it then we already have it but do not realize that we have it. When we give away what we desire, we will see that we have always had it.

If we want to see something blossom in to our life, we start giving it away. If we want to experience courage, engage in a courageous activity. Then we will manifest, or *realize*, those aspects of our self that were latent or hidden. If we want friendship, be a friend. We bloom where we are planted; we start wherever we find our self. It is this spiritual principle that is expressed in this part of the Oz story. It is what is realized in the 12th Gate of Service.

But what about Dorothy? The wizard said that he could take Dorothy home since he was from the land of "E Pluribus Unum," which means, "Out of the many - One." This is also printed on the U.S. one-dollar bill, to symbolize the United States of America. For our purpose, it speaks to the fact that individuals are many expressions of the One.

In his closing statements to his constituents, the wizard goes on to state that he is "going to the other side to confer, converse and otherwise hobnob with his brother wizards." Maybe this is a hint as to what we will be doing on the "other" side of the veil.

Just before the hot air balloon ascends into the air, Toto jumps from it. Dorothy follows him by jumping out of it too. So she misses her opportunity to return home. This is what so many of us do. Often, we allow those whom we love to hold us back from going "home" because we want them to come too. Heaven just wouldn't be heaven without them, right? Unfortunately, this delays our return. Many spiritual philosophies teach us that these types of attachments may hold us back.

Rather than ascending to Heaven, we might choose to stay in the Emerald City to do service work or to help others. But consider that, at times, we might have to do service work that takes us back into the dark forest. We may end up at the witch's castle, not knowing why or how we got there. Fear not. But listen closely to our True Power for guidance and power, and all will be even better than before.

Going back into the dark forest will not be the same experience. We have tools, gifts and power that we did not have before we passed through the Gates. But as Glinda warned 'stay tight inside' the slippers or we will be at the witch's mercy.

Whether to return or not is a personal choice that cannot be made until we get to that point in our journey. Many ascended masters have chosen to stay close to the illusion in order to help others return to reality. Others have not. There is no "right" or "wrong" choice.

When Glinda appears, Dorothy asks her for help once again. Glinda says, "You don't need help any longer. You've always had the power to go back." The scarecrow asks Glinda why Dorothy wasn't told this at the beginning of the journey. Glinda reveals that Dorothy wouldn't have believed her if she had been told that truth. Dorothy had to mature and develop beliefs of possibility in her journey on the yellow brick road.

The tin man asks Dorothy what she has learned from her experience in Oz. Dorothy responds: "I think that it wasn't enough just to want to see Aunty Em and Uncle Henry, and it's that, if I ever go looking for my heart's desire again, I won't look any further than in my own backyard because, if it isn't there, I haven't really lost it to begin with." In other words, everything she needed and wanted was already at home. She was *already* whole and complete.

In regards to returning home to reality, this is quite relevant. Aunty Em and Uncle Henry represent the feminine and masculine aspects of our Creator - Mother/Father God. These aspects are more or less mirrored in our earthly parents or guardians. We are never separate from our Creator. Separation is the illusion.

Here is a fascinating irony of the Oz parable. Recall at the beginning of the story where Dorothy is thinking about running away from home to save Toto from Mrs. Gulch. Did you notice that, after Dorothy leaves Oz and awakens back in Kansas, the issue of Toto's demise is never resolved? It might have been better if Dorothy had returned home initially without him. Then she could have worked out the problem for his safe return.

This situation represents emotional, intellectual, social, material and physical attachments that hold us back from evolving. Attachments are discussed heavily in Buddhism, Hinduism and other philosophies. Buddha, himself, walked away from his infant son. This is a deep issue that we must delve into with our True Power and trusted advisors. Our True Power exists outside of both time and space, so it can literally see the bigger picture of our life.

In the Oz story, Glinda tells Dorothy that all she needs to do to return home is to click the heels of her ruby slippers together three times. This might have different meanings for us. Only we know what our ruby slippers really are. This is the divine gifts which carry us down our yellow brick road.

For many people, the ruby slippers represent faith, or the desire for self-realization or actualization, or for our True Power. They could also represent our discipline, our Path, the Holy Spirit, our spirituality or our spiritual gifts. Likely, they support our purpose for incarnating into this illusion.

The slippers were given to Dorothy after her interaction with Glinda. Dorothy sought Glinda's guidance by asking her how she could get home. When Dorothy clicks her heels three times and awakens from her dream, she finds that she was *already* home. Her Aunty Em is there, lovingly pleading to her, "Wake up, honey. Wake up." - just like our True Power is doing with us all of the time.

All of Dorothy's loved ones who shared a part in her dream are present in the bedroom where she fell asleep. They were all a part of her (positive) ego in the dream. The lion represented her courage, the scarecrow represented her knowledge and the tin man represented her heart.

At the beginning of the Oz story, Glinda hugged Dorothy, just as Aunty Em might have done. Aunt Em was represented in the dream by Glinda, the good witch. Uncle Henry's father figure was partially represented in the wizard (but mainly by the travelling Professor) as the masculine God. He is God; Glinda is Goddess - the Divine masculine and the Divine feminine.

So Dorothy is now home, safe and sound, as we will be someday. Similarly, we will awaken to our great family of Beings who will greet us as we awaken. They currently support us on our journey. Like Dorothy, we will relay to them this far-fetched story of our very "real" adventure.

As we try to convince them that we really were in another place, they will laugh adoringly as they remind us it is simply not possible to ever leave home. They will assure us that we have been home all along. And we always will be. We were simply sleeping.

We will gratefully reply, "There's no place like home."

~~~~~~~~~~~~~~~~~~~~~~~~~~~~~~~~~~~~~

All the world is a stage and
we are the actors

- W. Shakespeare

~~~~~~~~~~~~~~~~~~~~~~~~~~~~~~~~~~~~~

Why Do We Love Drama?

The Wizard of Oz is a drama. It's a mythology that conveys some of the secrets of life and of spirituality. These are "positive" uses for drama. They create a parable that reaches beyond our left brain logical thinking and grasps the genius of the non-linear right brain. Stories sink into the sub-conscious (accessed mainly by right-brain) bypassing the ego (accessed mainly by left-brain). There is very good reason to love drama, especially when it contains lessons that initiate and support our awakening. Indeed, the very experience we are living is a big drama. It is nothing but an illusion. Thus, stories speak to us on an incredibly deep level. On the other hand, another meaning, use and word for drama is *negativity*.

The most popular dramas today are soap operas. In a soap opera, there must be a "protagonist" and an "antagonist" – a hero and a villain. They are filled with so many lessons that support distrust, ego, dishonesty, pride, thoughtlessness, fear, self-centeredness, hurt and disillusionment. Always ask how a situation supports our awakening. The Merriam-Webster online dictionary defines the word *negativity* as follows:

"Harmful or bad, not wanted,"

"Thinking about the bad qualities of someone or something,"

"Thinking that a bad result will happen,"

"Not hopeful or optimistic"

In order to awaken from the Nightmare of Nowhere, we need a solid understanding of the fact that negativity is a hallmark of the nightmare. There is heaviness in the nightmare that doesn't exist Elsewhere. We might be able to feel this in the pit of our stomach and in the weight on our shoulders. Is it any wonder people hunch over in old age? They have been living too long in the Nightmare. There is nothing "wrong" with negativity. It is not "bad." Indeed nothing is "bad." But is it our preference?

The philosophy behind *A Course in Miracles* (ACIM) teaches that, when we are not awake, we are literally thinking nothing, doing nothing and planning nothing with nobody. This is the mental state of the people who are living in the Nightmare of Nowhere. A racing mind is often called "monkey-mind." This mindset and sense of heaviness are a two indications that we are roaming about in the Nightmare.

The 1965 Beatles song, *Nowhere Man*, seems very poignant, considering this discussion. It seems that the Beatles already understood this in the 1960s. ACIM first appeared that very same year. But surely this is just a coincidence. Here's part of their song:

He's a real Nowhere Man,
Sitting in his Nowhere Land,
Making all his Nowhere plans
For nobody
Doesn't have a point of view,
Knows not where he's going to,
Isn't he a bit like you and me?

The great news is that Nowhere is a place of illusion, so nobody really does anything to anyone there. We live in our own universe, which exists in a state of our mind that is not real. We interact with our projections of people while we live in our universe. However, their universe exists in a state of *their* mind that is also not real. Both are illusions. So no one can ever actually harm anyone. That is the reason we can forgive and be forgiven - instantly. Nothing ever happened that needed to be forgiven.

Then why do people believe that they can be harmed in this illusion? Because, long-long ago, our mind fragmented. It projected a world that contains separate physical bodies and things that seem could be "harmed". Nowhere is only a perception of an external world. But it all exists in our mind. It's a dream in which we perceive our self and others performing actions to and for others, both "good" and "bad." An action or thought is either loving or it is a *call* for love. The opposite of love is *unloving.* But it is really *harmful if nothing is happening and we are all eternal beings who are whole and complete in reality?* Love has no opposite in reality.

Nowhere is a stage for a big drama – a theatrical play. The drama in which we live is like a big soap opera. This begs the question, "Why do we love dramatic stories so much?" This big drama is a way of experiencing all of the possible possibilities. In Hinduism, it is called Lila – the play of Brahma. But, as a group, we have experienced all of the possible realities. We have traveled exceedingly far, over the rainbow. Now it is time to head toward Home.

Perhaps we have wondered why we see little children starving and what kind of terrible god created this illusion? I hate to tell you this – we did. Take note. This piece of truth will free you from the Nightmare. Many religions purport that this is a dream. More specifically, it is *our* dream.

Think about it. Our perception is our reality. It governs how and what we see in front of us. Luckily, just by deciding to see everything from a loving perspective, we can change our perception from a fear-based one to a love-based one. A loving perspective includes the understanding that the laws that govern our universe are loving, fair and understandable.

But, before we can find, accept and understand the reasons as to why and how situations happen in our outer world, we need to 'clean our house.' Just make a start. We can do this by working through the 12 Rainbow Gates that are partially described in this book (see Rainbow Gates Series workbooks for full instructions) so that we become clear enough to hear, see and accept the answers that are sent to us from our True Power. They are there. But we must prepare to see these answers. Some call it 'purification.'

The whole point of these 12 Gates is to establish a relationship with our True Power and be restored to our true Self. The truth will set us free. But first it may make us livid. We might be mad already. But, if we want the truth and we do our research, we will find it.

Harm is an illusion. Only the body and ego can be hurt. They are not eternal and therefore not real. Nothing real can be threatened. Our essence is real, but our ego is not. Our ego is attached to its thinking; its roles; its possessions; its plans. If we identify with our ego's perspective, then we will feel its pain when its plans do not work out. The pain will reveal the attachment that we must release.

The negative ego is an egomaniac with an inferiority complex. When the ego thinks negatively, we will think negatively too - but only if we identify with it. We might believe that we have "bad" luck. But, no. That's our ego's thinking and we are identifying with its idea about bad luck.

We are amazing beyond words. Nothing can be withheld from us, except *by* us. That is how powerful we are. So, if we wholly believe that we are always taken care of, we will allow the Universe to provide for us. Get out of its way. This is part of the meaning of "Thy will, not mine, be done." Our True Power desires the best for us, but our ego does not. It is not the will of our True Power that we feel fearful; it is the will of our ego. Only *we* can prevent the Universe from providing for us - by identifying with the ego and its ideologies. Furthermore, the same holds true for those we desperately want to help.

Even though it wanted them at one time, the ego doesn't appreciate the house and the car, the job and the boss, the kids and the spouse, or even the dog. It will always find something "wrong" with them. Again, if we identify with the ego, instead of seeking another perspective, we will believe that the ego's perspective is *our* perspective.

We live under a set of Universal Laws. One key to working with these laws is to appreciate and feel good about what we have right now. Then, and only then, will we be able to attract something better. When we live in the Nightmare of Nowhere, we must learn to appreciate and express gratitude for what we have, who we are and what we are doing *now*. The feeling of gratitude is especially powerful in manifesting prosperity and abundance. The longer we focus on an idea while we are in gratitude, the faster it manifests.

If we get something that *seems* to be better than what we have now, without first appreciating what we have, ultimately, we do not feel any better. Eventually, it manifests similar problems and we sink into our previous mindset. But, if we practice enjoying what we have, that is the state we continue to experience when it's time to receive something new. We choose what state of mind we want to experience, here and now. So we need to start appreciating what we have now. Then, we may move from something good to something 'better.'

If we cannot find anything redeeming about someone, then, at least, believe that they are one of our greatest teachers. They might catalyze a nightmarish situation in our life. But that is their job – to motivate our awakening. Generally, life contracts for these scenarios are made before we are born. Now we must figure out what they are trying to teach us because they are helping us to find our way out of the Nightmare.

They may be showing us how to love the unlovable. They may be giving us the opportunity to forgive the unforgiveable. They may be giving us the motivation to see through this illusion by removing the illusion of control. Whatever it is, it feels like hell at first. This is our opportunity to transform hell into heaven. For that, we can be grateful. If we can pray for them we are on our way.

We know that we have left the Nightmare of Nowhere when we start appreciating what we have and enjoying what we do. We love who we are and we accept our self in spite of our perceived faults. We are our own best friend. We see the spark of God in others and our self.

Certainly, we do not talk poorly about our self or gossip about others. When we talk about others, it is with joy and admiration, or at least it is with sincerity. We start to wake up not fearing the day. The battle begins to fade away.

Eventually, we look forward to each and every day, and we find our self in "the flow." We enjoy the company of others. We are much more productive in less time. We do everything that we need to do, with energy and time to spare.

The Promises of the *Alcoholics Anonymous* (AA) program are astounding. Since the mid-1900s, they have made a standing *promise* that, if we incorporate their philosophies, we are transformed. The following is taken from the AA *Big Book*, which refers to working the 9th Step in the AA program:

If we are painstaking about this phase of our development, we will be amazed before we are halfway through. We are going to know a new freedom and a new happiness. We will not regret the past nor wish to shut the door on it. We will comprehend the word serenity and we will know peace. No matter how far down the scale we have gone, we will see how our experience can benefit others. That feeling of uselessness and self-pity will disappear. We will lose interest in selfish things and gain interest in our fellows. Self-seeking will slip away. Our whole attitude and outlook on life will change. Fear of people and economic insecurity will leave us. We will intuitively know how to handle situations, which used to baffle us. We will suddenly realize that God is doing for us what we could not do for our self. Are these extravagant promises? We think not. They are being fulfilled among us - sometimes quickly, sometimes slowly. They will always materialize if we work for them[6].

We can choose the time at which we walk out of the Nightmare of Nowhere. But, if we delay after we are 'called' our pain turns to suffering and increases in time. In order to stay on the Path, we must walk out into the light. As it is said, "When the pain of staying the same is greater than the pain of changing, we will change." So, in this case, pain is our friend. We thank it for doing its job.

People who are in recovery must grow spiritually if they want to remain in recovery. This is true for all spiritual people. By suffering severe consequences, many addicts are blessed with the pain of desperation. It can make their choice really simple. We are pushed by pain until we are pulled by the vision. There's no "right" or "wrong." We decide when enough is enough. Time is the only thing we can waste. At some point, we all will do the work that is described here. So why postpone something of such great importance? Later never comes.

[6] *Reprinted from the book Alcoholics Anonymous (The Big Book) with permission of A.A. World Services, Inc.*

A "dry drunk" is somebody who is not currently drinking, but who is miserable, nevertheless. It is a slight misconception that a dry drunk is somebody who has not worked the 12 Steps of AA. Negativity and lack are attitudes that can manifest anytime if vigilance isn't maintained. For addicts and alcoholics substance dependency is their 'calling.' It's time to get serious.

For others, this manifests in a variety of ways. We have all known people who are miserable and who are attached to their martyrdom, accepting little or no responsibility for the state of their life. The crazy old codger; the neighborhood gossip; the cat hoarder; the compulsive gambler; the drama queen, etc. These are extreme stereotypical examples, but most live in a quiet desperation. Countless live the rest of their lives unaware they are being called to awaken.

Some of the most common issues people have are centered on money, career (purpose), health, relationships and happiness. On the other hand, many of the spiritual philosophies that incorporate the Universal Laws of Attraction tend to bypass the more serious problems that people have, such as codependency, trauma, child abuse, domestic violence, harassment, poverty, health problems, addiction and alcoholism, as well as other issues, such as depression and anxiety.

Bypassing the introspective, spiritually defining and purification phases of self-inquiry can be a problem for people who are trying to implement the Universal Laws. The philosophy behind these laws is that we will attract into our life the people, places, situations and things that resonate with our beliefs, attitudes, thoughts and feelings. Believe it or not, the Laws of Attraction are responding to our vibrational frequencies in every single moment. At this very moment, we are sowing seeds for tomorrow's harvest. What we thought about yesterday is what we will see today.

Some people call this *magnetic* attraction because there is mounting scientific evidence by quantum physicists that these laws are mathematically arguable as magnetizing. There is a humorous anecdote that states, "If we see three rude people in a day; then we need to adjust our attitude" because the world is reflecting our own state of mind. Pay attention, the world is literally our reflection. Thank goodness and be grateful. What a great system for awareness. It gives us endless chances to improve our self and our life.

No one is exempt from the Laws of Attraction. So there is good reason for learning to use them effectively. Affirmations are a form of prayer. But people often find that their affirmations seem ineffective. Their past subconscious issues, like worthlessness and shame, interfere with their manifestations because they do not know that the world is only a reflection of their beliefs. Hence, they have not let go of old ideas about God and spirituality, family and parents, trauma and powerlessness, society and status, career and responsibilities, money and sex.

The 12 Rainbow Gates can be used to address issues that are interfering with the manifestation of these old ideas. Furthermore, this spiritual groundwork gives a solid foundation for successfully advancing with other spiritual philosophies, as well. Think of it as the Gates to our spirituality. Any spiritual Path will only be enhanced by these 12 Gates.

I wish I had known long ago about the dire importance of living gratefully and joyfully. Like so many others, I was grateful to be relieved of my addictions (with the exception of coffee, work and technology, of course). But, unfortunately, there was an underlying feeling that I didn't have the *right* to fully enjoy my life. So, it is no surprise that I was diagnosed with major clinical depression in the year 2002. More accurately, I was disabled with it. This had been the case since I was very young.

My experience is that, if they are left unaddressed, subconscious issues can unexpectedly raise their hideous heads. Codependency, fear, depression and other issues may needlessly delay spiritual progress for an indefinite period.

If we are fortunate in that we have not been touched by addiction and codependency issues, then we probably have not had much reason to engage in the 12 Steps of AA and other similar programs. But, for those who are in recovery, a program that is specifically focused on developing an attitude of gratitude and joy, and a strong relationship with our True Power is priceless.

Because of their transformational experience, many people who are in recovery look back with gratitude on the fact that they were compelled to join a recovery program. Unfortunately, many people do not even consider attending these meetings, due to the stigma that surrounds them.

Indeed, we must be willing to look with the light of love at the dark corners of our mind and heart. It is true that only the courageous pass this way. But, as a spiritual warrior, bravery is our hallmark. If we are reading this, it's true. If it were easy, everyone would do it. It's not easy, but it is worth it.

If we are dissatisfied with our life, take action. In some ways, we are the power behind our True Power. It needs our permission to act on our behalf. It cannot violate our free will. So, in truth, we can do things that our True Power cannot do (at least without the media getting wind of it). Some of the things we can do include:

- Find a pen and a piece of paper, and write.
- Consult with others.
- Read a relevant book.
- Get to a spiritual or Rainbow Gates meeting.

- Serve others.
- Bathe, eat, pray, meditate, etc.

Our True Power is supportive of us. It gives us guidance if we listen. But it cannot do these things for us. So these are our responsibilities. In this way we are the power that is working with our True Power. Hence, the saying "God helps those who help themselves."

On the other hand, our True Power will do for us what we cannot do for our self, that is, if we let it. So, for example, if someone is illiterate, their True Power might find someone who will teach them to read. If a problem is not directly or immediately resolvable, their True Power will give serenity to accept the situation. If someone cannot stop themselves from giving in to a compulsion, their True Power might influence a friend to call to distract them. I have heard many variations of the story of someone who does their best to be respectful to a co-worker who bullies them. The person says a prayer for their coworker and shortly thereafter, they leave.

Our True Power works better for us when we know how to work with it. We don't interfere in our True Power's business. We must do our part, but we must also release our True Power so it can to do its part. This way, we empower it so that, when it is free to be the Super Power that it is, we will become super-powered as well.

We become spiritually fit. Miracles happen. Our lives flow.

~~~~~~~~~~~~~~~~~~~~~~~~~~~~~~~~~~~~~~~

"Miracles should happen regularly. If they are not something has gone wrong."
- ACIM

~~~~~~~~~~~~~~~~~~~~~~~~~~~~~~~~~~~~~~~

About the 12 Rainbow Gates

"Having had a spiritual awakening..."A spiritual awakening[7] is the point of the 12 Steps. A reprieve of an insidious condition is just the byproduct of a spiritual awakening albeit a pleasant one.

The original 12 Steps of the *Alcoholics Anonymous* program were designed to complement almost any spiritual program. Parts of the 12 Steps have been removed and added to in order to bring out their highest use. It has been a labor love acting as a translator for spiritual seekers in the new millennia. I have endeavored to reveal the truest and highest meaning in each Step that might be hidden to the newcomer. But I do not assume that I have the best or last word on this matter.

The 12 Rainbow Gates are not meant to replace the Steps. However, the 12 Rainbow Gates address the existential dilemmas that are seemingly brought on by awakening in the Nightmare of Nowhere. If we have a problem with a substance addiction or codependency, it is highly recommended to focus on the set of 12 Steps which specifically addresses it. Later, when the addictive problem is in remission, it may be safe to employ the 12 Rainbow Gates. A solid ascetic foundation is a must.

---

[7] © *Alcoholics Anonymous,* Fourth Edition, page 59, reprinted with permission of Alcoholics Anonymous World Services, Inc.

My husband completed his last round of the Steps in one week and has never felt the need to work them again. However, it took me three years to complete my last round. I have worked through them several times, with amazing results. I have overcome pill addiction, alcoholism and eating disorders. I have addressed every type of abuse and co-dependency. Although these are continuing practices, I have experienced a miraculous transformation. Everyone must decide for themselves what is right for them.

The last time I worked through the Gates, I did so to overcome my disabling grief, depression and the guilt I carried over the circumstances of my children. They suffered untold abuse from which I could not extricate them. Although I fought in court for 13 years, I did not see them for nine of those years. I had an existential crisis and was classified as disabled with depression. For years, I wanted to die - almost every day. My problem was no longer any addiction; but, an existential crisis. I felt powerless. But, fortunately, I was mistaken. This version of the Gates is how I inwardly viewed the 12 Steps due to my other spiritual studies. Here is a quote from the AA Big Book:

There is a solution. Almost none of us liked the self-searching, the leveling of our pride, the confession of shortcomings which the process requires for its successful consummation. But we saw that it really worked in others, and we had come to believe in the hopelessness and futility of life as we had been living it. When, therefore, we were approached by those in whom the problem had been solved, there was nothing left for us but to pick up the simple kit of spiritual tools laid at our feet. We have found much of heaven and we have been rocketed into a fourth dimension of existence of which we had not even dreamed.[8]

Work through the 12 Rainbow Gates as we are led to, but hold them sacred. As with any endeavor, we get out of the Gates what we put into them. In other words, "it works if we work it." They should be worked wholly, in order and not in part. Once we start we have opened Pandora's Box and cannot return to our life as before. Our eyes will have been opened and we cannot return to blindness.

We cannot be on the fence especially after the 3rd Gate of Decision without increasing pain. This is just fair warning. *Realizing Emerald City* is only the introduction to the 12 Rainbow Gates. To assist with our ascent through these Gates use the companion workbooks series entitled *The Rainbow Gates Workbooks*.

---

[8] © *Alcoholics Anonymous*, Fourth Edition, page 25, reprinted with permission of Alcoholics Anonymous World Services, Inc.

~~~~~~~~~~~~~~~~~~~~~~~~~~~~

"I tried to control unmanageability… It didn't work."-Anonymous

~~~~~~~~~~~~~~~~~~~~~~~~~~~~

Gate 1: Illusion

We admitted we felt powerless. We ceased fighting.

We come into the 12 Rainbow Gates *feeling* powerless. Our life *seems* to be unmanageable. This is because the first of the 12 Gates is the Gate of Illusion. But we are ready to let go of that illusion now. Correct?

In this 1st Gate, the concept of having to admit powerlessness was removed from the original 1st Step of AA[9] and was replaced with the phrase, "felt powerless." Furthermore, the phrase, "became unmanageable," was removed and "We ceased fighting" was added. The spirit of surrender is maintained from the original step.

The original 1st Step affirmed powerlessness and unmanageability. According to Abraham Hicks, Magenta Pixie, Bashar and other well-known spiritual teachers, affirmations are a form of prayer. In other words, we do not affirm powerlessness and unmanageability in the Gates. If we have power, any power, then by definition, we are not powerless. We are simply not using our power correctly, or we do not know where our power lies.

Let's use an analogy of a dark room... There is darkness in that room. So we have to open the window

---

[9] © *Alcoholics Anonymous,* Fourth Edition, page 59, reprinted with permission of Alcoholics Anonymous World Services, Inc.

or flip the light switch to illuminate it. But we are upset because we keep bumping into things. Maybe we don't know where the window is. This is simply unawareness. Or maybe we think that we should be able to see in the dark. This is simply distorted thinking for a human (but not for a cat).

Either way, we certainly will *feel* powerless in this situation, but there is a simple solution. In either case, we just need understanding or acceptance of the circumstances. Focus on where our power is and flip on the light switch. Our life is not unmanageable. It might *seem* to be unmanageable, but the laws of the Universe are working in perfect order in our life. We are getting results, just not the ones we want.

When Dorothy landed in Oz, she realized that she was not in Kansas anymore. She realized that, what she was seeing in the land of Oz was not normal. She was not delusional. She passed through the Gate of Illusion.

The very home she had run away from was now where Dorothy longed to be. It really doesn't matter what our life circumstances are if we don't feel joyful and grateful for them. We can own a Mercedes-Benz and the biggest, most beautiful home in the most desirable neighborhood. But, if that doesn't make us happy, does it really matter?

Most people refer to wealthy people as "abundant" and "prosperous." But, if those same wealthy individuals don't *feel* prosperous, their wealth is not making them joyful.

Princess Diana said she felt imprisoned. She suffered from both an eating disorder and an image disorder. She desperately felt the need to meet the public's ideals of her. She felt great pressure to be perfect. I can go on, but the point is that fame and fortune do not necessarily make people happy. Maybe we've heard the cliché about the difference between a rich man and a poor man. The rich man knows that money won't make him happy.

In the 1st Gate, when we admit that we feel powerless, we open the doors for change. No one can admit this for us. Admission of the feeling of powerlessness is, in itself, healing. It means that we are conscious of a limiting feeling, belief or attitude.

In the 1st Gate, we do not say, "We admitted we were powerless,"[10] as is stated in the original 12 Steps of the AA program. We are not powerless. Nonetheless, at times, we might *feel* powerless. This is a far-reaching difference and a potent one. Note: if we have any kind of power, we cannot by definition be powerless. How can we, Child of the Creator, be powerless?

It is important to be mindful of when we *feel* powerless because this indicates a problem. Ironically,

---

[10] © *Alcoholics Anonymous,* Fourth Edition, page 59, reprinted with permission of Alcoholics Anonymous World Services, Inc.

when read another way, the feeling of powerlessness is a lie in itself. It is an untruth. But, if we believe that we are powerless, we will continue to manifest an experience of powerlessness. What is most interesting is that we will be right because we are always right. It is *our* universe. Our belief is that powerful.

Belief in powerlessness might have served many people in the original 12 Steps of AA. However, as the 12 Steps program says, "God will constantly disclose more to you and to us."[11] The revelation is that "admission of powerlessness"[12] at a certain point is not only unnecessary; it can be a potential block to receiving *more* power. There is a misperception that the 12 Step originators had a problem with personal power. Nothing could be farther from the truth.

The 11th Step entails that we seek the power to carry out the will of our True Power. In the AA *Big Book*, it is written that "lack of power that was our dilemma."[13] It also states, "As we felt new power flow in, as we enjoyed peace of mind, as we discovered we could face life successfully, as we became conscious of His Presence,

---

[11] © *Alcoholics Anonymous*, Fourth Edition, page 164, reprinted with permission of Alcoholics Anonymous World Services, Inc.

[12] Admission of powerlessness over certain things such as alcohol may be appropriate. But it is still a matter of focusing attention. If we are still trying to exert power when it has definitive negative consequences then it is simply self-will. Our True Power is showing us it is time to relinquish something.

[13] © *Alcoholics Anonymous*, Fourth Edition, page 45, reprinted with permission of Alcoholics Anonymous World Services, Inc.

we began to lose our fear of today, tomorrow or the hereafter. We were reborn."[14] Furthermore, when explaining how we could better align our will with the will of our True Power, the AA *Big Book* reads, "we can exercise our will power along this line all we wish; it is the proper use of the will."

This is not *censure* of power. On the contrary, the AA *Big Book* actually acknowledges the *need* for power. Indeed, when we gain alignment with the will of our True Power as we work through the 12 Gates, we gain power.

What if we learned how to use our power correctly, instead of naïvely using it against our self? Not knowing how our True Power works is like getting a new telephone with all of the gadgets on it, but without any instructions. It can be very frustrating. We hang up on a customer by accident and don't know how to dial them back. Or the alarm wakes us up in the middle of the night. Or we don't know how to turn on the WIFI connection to hear our favorite songs. We just want to return the device to the store. This is how we react if we do not understand how our True Power operates.

Any complex instrument that we don't know how to use is useless, frustrating and sometimes downright dangerous. But our True Power is infinitely more complex

---

[14] © *Alcoholics Anonymous,* Fourth Edition, page 63, reprinted with permission of Alcoholics Anonymous World Services, Inc.

than a telephone. We and our True Powers are amazing technologies.

Luckily, there are simple "instructions" for living a super-powered life in which love is experienced and miracles happen regularly. By staying in contact with our True Power, we will learn how to work with it and how to expand upon it. We could even say that we will get regular "updates and downloads."

We don't need to be burning with love to start working on the 1st Gate. We just need to start somewhere and have somewhere to start. We might have reached a point where we can no longer continue in the same manner physically, mentally and spiritually, due to the pain.

It is when we are "being" and not "doing" that we become willing to surrender. Surrender is not giving up; it is not giving in to a terrible force that will torment us. It is ceasing to fight and allowing something else to help us. A drowning man cannot be saved while he is flailing about. He must cease fighting. Surrender is an open mindedness and a willingness to accept help and mentoring.

The fact that we feel powerless is a symptom of spiritual sickness. When our life seems unmanageable is also a symptom of spiritual illness. In the Nightmare of Nowhere, these are the lies that are fed to us. Nowhere will always tell us, "You are powerless." But we are only *feeling* powerless; our life only *seems* to be unmanageable.

If we believe in powerlessness it will lead to unending crises. We will experience a snowball effect. It will keep compounding itself into more and more feelings of powerlessness. All we have to do is admit that there are these symptoms: feelings of powerlessness and unmanageability.

This brings them up from the subconscious level where they have been hiding and can then be healed. Spiritual illness is like a virus that is contained deep within a computer's system. But no one can really determine where it is rooted. It doesn't matter where it stems from initially. Just allow it to surface so it can be eliminated. Otherwise, what we resist will persist.

Addiction is a spiritual disease, as well. This particular spiritual disease might not have manifested as addiction in our life, but it's an infirmity that impacts our life, nonetheless. It affects every area of our life. No place in our heart, mind or body is too sacred to be exempt from its effects, given enough time.

We may have found that there are aspects of our life in which our behavior seems to be chaotic or compulsive. Maybe we work a little too much. Western society deeply rewards those who turn their lives over to their work. Most people don't consider this to be much of a problem. So, we will get little support from our boss in whittling down this character trait. As a matter of fact, it's considered commendable in most social circles, in spite of the fact workaholism is a serious problem.

It is up to us to decide what challenges or issues we want to address within the Rainbow Gates. We can use them to address anything we desire, even health issues. Once we are released from a trait, no matter how insignificant it may seem we find the wellspring that the trait was holding back – both light and dark. It is similar to the boy who put his thumb into the dike in order to prevent a flood. When the thumb is removed, memories and feelings flood in. Moreover, the muck will come out before the clear fresh water of our spirit does. Hang in there. This is normal.

The spiritual part of this disease is *negative* self-centeredness. This is not a constructive act, like self-care. It manifests in the form of self-centered fear, which is the fear that we will lose something that we have, or that we won't receive something that we desire.

This does not mean that, in this lifetime, we will not lose things. It just means that we will not *fear* the loss of them. This does not mean that we will get everything we desire, but we will not *worry* about whether or not we will get it.

If we live in the state of joy, as opposed to happiness, losing something will not be a fearful event. Joy is not swayed by events and happenings. Similarly, if we live in a state of gratitude for what we have, there is nothing that we will need in order to feel joyful. We may prefer it but we won't *need* it.

Happiness is a temporary state that is based on happenstance, whereas joy is a continual state of "being." This is how we can tell the difference between joy and happiness. One is fleeting and the other is an almost completely permanent state. We nurture fleeting moments of happiness so that, in time, we may switch over into a perennial state of joy by stitching moments together - one after another. Practice being joyful for no reason, especially when there is every reason for the contrary.

If we cannot be joyful, then we practice gratitude because everything is working for our spiritual progress. Everything is happening *for* us. Now we know we are making real progress. But, like it says in the AA, "Sometimes quickly, sometimes slowly."[15] Practicing self-acceptance and self-love is key.

It is important to remember that we are not at fault; we are not guilty for the state in which we exist. Guilt can only exist in the past and the past is not real. Guilt is a lie of the Nightmare of Nowhere. However, although we are not guilty for the state in which we exist, we *are* responsible to change it. Responsibility exists in

---

[15] © *Alcoholics Anonymous*, Fourth Edition, page 84, reprinted with permission of Alcoholics Anonymous World Services, Inc.

the present and that is where our power is - Now. Furthermore, we are the only ones who can initiate change in our self. We don't waste our power trying to change others. We don't change our behavior in order to change others. It doesn't work ultimately and we become miserable.

We have tried to transform our self on our own. But, initially, we do need the help of others to speed us along. Isolation, at this point, is a recipe for disaster. A problem cannot be solved from the same mind that created it. So, at the outset, our True Power reaches and teaches us through other people who understand the Path we are traveling.

Eventually, when several errors in our thinking have been corrected, we are able to safely trust our own mind again. It might be hard to admit that we need others. So, in order to keep moving forward, we considered joining a spiritual group. Who wants to be held to a group structure in life if they don't have to be? A person who desires to move to the next level of spiritual growth - that's who. A person who needs a deeper contact with their True Power - that's who. A person who is tired of living in the Nightmare of Nowhere - that's who.

Many of us have tried psychiatrists, exercise programs, medications, lovers, new philosophies or religions, new jobs or towns. However, the happiness that these things gave us was only temporary. Joy and gratitude eluded us.

In order for the Rainbow Gates to help, we incorporate them as a way of life that set us on solid footing for success and awakening. The foundation for these Gates is that we admit that we *feel* powerless over something in our life and that we cease fighting anything and anyone. We let go of all reservations.

The basis of the 12 Gates is a tried and true method for changing people's lives. As is wonderfully stated in the AA *Big Book*, "Some of us have tried to hold on to our old ideas and the result was **nil** until we let go absolutely."[16] Letting go of our reservations means that we choose to be honest, open-minded and willing. This is the H.O.W. of any program.

If we do not believe in this program, believe that I believe. As an addiction specialist, spiritual seeker and recovering person, I have witnessed thousands of miracles. I also experienced miracles in my life.

Before we go through the 1st Gate, we may feel fear or uncertainty. Help is available but can only come when it is sincerely desired and asked for. The 1st Gate can be frightening. Nonetheless it is the touchstone of freedom and it is freedom that is our goal, not security.

---

[16] © *Alcoholics Anonymous,* Fourth Edition, page 58, reprinted with permission of Alcoholics Anonymous World Services, Inc.

The reason why some prisons are called "maximum security" is because they are very secure. They restrict our freedom. But they do provide healthcare, three meals a day and a bed. Some prefer this situation over freedom. No judgment; it's a valid choice. Of course, not everyone who has been in prison feels this way, but some people will actually create a reason to be sent back to prison. Freedom is not worth the price to them.

In truth, what we are really afraid of is not failure or the feeling of powerlessness – it is our power. We are incredibly powerful. That is what no one in the Nightmare of Nowhere wants us to know.

In Nowhere, there is press control. We can see the mirror of this phenomenon in our daily lives. The news desires only to cover chaos. Many leading psychologist and spiritualists now advocate that we not read or watch the news. It is not worth our sanity.

By admitting that we feel powerless and ceasing to fight we have opened the door for our True Power to aid us in our journey. This might be our first trip outside of the Nightmare of Nowhere. But freedom does not have to be frightening. Soon, we find that we are able to approach the Rainbow Gates and start our journey through them.

The Nightmare of Nowhere does have several checkpoints at which we must stop before we can be released, however. Many, who have traveled by airplane, know that checkpoints can be tricky sometimes.

Speaking of emotions, there is a saying that "what goes up must come down." What does that mean? When we reach an extreme state of excitement, we often crash into despair to the same degree. While intensive learning is taking place, we often experience something like this emotional roller coaster ride, as we toggle between Nowhere and Somewhere. The good news is that the higher dimensional feelings of joy, inspiration and love have no such boomerang effect. The bad news is that we need to do the work to get there. Commit to memory, "It works if we work it."

If we follow this program closely, we will safely make it through and out of the nightmare to our freedom. We will be heading to the Happy Dream. From there, we will be more capable of choosing where we go and how long we will stay. The Rainbow Gates program gives us the tools to do just that. We have studied the hardest Gate - the Gate of Illusion. Now let's move on to the 2nd Gate.

~~~~~~

"If you can't believe then believe that I believe."

-Dr. Greene

~~~~~~

Gate 2: Trust

We came to believe that cooperation with our True Power and Universal Laws would restore us to sanity.

The Gate of Trust asks us to reflect on our relationship with our True Power as a cooperative one, not one in which it has power over us. But, although we do not give our life over without the ability to take it back at any time, unfortunately, it is very easy to take back control of our lives in a negative way. This is called the Gate of Distrust. Entering it causes *unnecessary* suffering.

This 2nd Gate of Trust is of vast importance because it is the foundation of trust. It's called the Gate of Trust because it requires that we trust our True Power. In so doing, we discover what capacities it does and does not possess. We determine the conditions under which it can help us. It will not give us what we think we want - if it is going to hurt us. A baby might want to play with a pair of scissors, but a wise parent will distract the infant. Likewise, we cannot judge what is best for us from our limited perspective. Accordingly, our True Power is the key to our sanity.

In the Gate of Trust we will either return to a childhood faith, through which we will re-establish a relationship with our True Power, or we will build a relationship with it from the ground up. If we do not understand how our True Power operates, we will hold unrealistic expectations, which will disappoint sooner or later. This is akin to a communication problem in a relationship. But, when we have put time and effort into building our relationship with our True Power, then we will be confident that our True Power deserves our trust.

When Dorothy became enamored by Glinda, the "good" witch, she passed through the 2nd Gate. Dorothy admired Glinda and instantly took a liking to her. She looked to her for help when the wicked witch appeared, and then for guidance as to the Way home. Basically, she had faith in Glinda. She trusted her. That is the basis of the 2nd Gate – the Gate of Trust.

When we have completed the 1st Gate, we may be left feeling ungrounded and needing direction. So the 2nd Gate requires that we attempt to understand how we may work harmoniously within our spiritual world. Essentially, we must leave no stone unturned in our quest for a relationship with our True Power and in the understanding of the laws under which it operates. Indeed, many people do not think that their True Power is actually *bound* by laws. Nothing could be further from the truth.

This 2nd Gate is my favorite, as it is for many people. It's deeper than it looks at first glance and there are many parts to it. Working through this Gate is usually a very magical time. Many beautiful things begin to happen. It is a True Power's way of making an impression on us. Nowadays, I often say, "Oh, that's my

True Power showing off again." I can almost hear my True Power's laughter. It can be this easy when we find a True Power who captivates our heart.

The phrase, "a Power greater than ourselves," was removed from the original 2nd Step of AA.[17] This is to open us up to the awareness that we are co-creators and partners with this Power. However, there may be a time when this Power really *feels* greater, because it can see the bigger picture and can do things that we cannot do.

It is in the material realm that we can do things that our True Power cannot do. It is us who drives a car; it is us who brushes our teeth. If we are a holographic microcosm of our Creator, don't we contain all of the same parts?

This Gate is meant to support the idea that we have our own knowledge and concept of our True Power and of the Universal laws under which it operates. This doesn't mean that we are necessarily masters at applying those laws. However, we will be spending quite a bit of time perfecting our application of them. Therefore, we must believe in them.

To believe in them we need a working idea of them. It is important not to reinvent the wheel here. That's one way that others, who have preceded us spiritually, can help us. Put another way, we start out

---

[17] (© *Alcoholics Anonymous*, Fourth Edition, page 59, reprinted with permission of Alcoholics Anonymous World Services, Inc.

with the basic framework of our True Power, and then, as we change, it changes too. It becomes experiential *knowing,* rather than just intellectual *believing.* But we must make a start, however small. We refine our belief systems along the way, but the core concepts need to be put in place. We do our homework.

If we do not believe that this great Power can help us, it won't matter if we think it is all just fairytales about how that Power will give us our heart's desire. We must trust to have results. Likewise, if we believe in a judgmental "gotcha" God that will strike us down for every little mistake we make, we cannot return to peace of mind[18]. So this is the Gate at which we must research, investigate and seek out the qualities of our True Power.

If we attend AA or NA meetings, at first we may not believe what the other members say about the miracles and the coincidences that are occurring in their lives. But, as we continue to hear about the wonders that are happening to them, we come to believe that our True Power is working on our behalf as well. We are nurturing our faith here, but our True Power will not disappoint if we take this Gate sincerely. If we believe that our True Power can restore us to sanity, it will get we through some seemingly impossible situations.

The 2nd Gate is the point at which we must decide what the word *sanity* truly means to us. Some people

---

[18] Peace of mind is an aspect of sanity.

feel good about having a place to go every day. To them, that is sanity. Others live spontaneously and would never consider working a steady eight-hour job. Still others strive to live mostly in the realm of the extreme. Maybe they enjoy skydiving, which is a behavior that other people consider to be quite insane.

What is sanity anyway? At first, it didn't sound very desirable to many of us. We have a great deal of margin when forming our definition of it. Let's return to the Merriam-Webster dictionary. The word *sanity* is defined as "the condition of being, based on reason or sound judgment" or "the condition of being sane." The dictionary definition for the word *sane* is "having a healthy mind." The word *sanity* was retained in this Gate because it is a word that means "wisdom," "reason," "understanding," "good sense," "mental health" and "stability." Essentially, it implies "right mind," which is key in the attainment of a joyful life.

This is our universe and it is our True Power that is operating within the Universal laws to which we individually subscribe. So we decide what we believe to be true because, whatever we believe, will be what we experience. Our beliefs will be refined as we move closer to truth.

Some people do not believe that they even have *access* to such power. For them, if something cannot be seen or measured, it does not exist. Not to worry.

Science is now illustrating that there are universal laws of physics, of nature and of the mind, which can be utilized very much like our True Power.

There really is no conflict here. We simply view our True Power as a version of our self that can do things for us that we cannot do for our self. This includes being able to see into the future, grant bliss, solve an impossible problem and even produce a miracle. It gains enormous power as the blocks to it are removed when it is accessed properly and regularly through prayer and meditation.

Many people do not think that this 2nd Gate is as important as the other Gates. Nothing could be further from the truth. We study this topic deeply, as if we were attempting a great escape from prison – because indeed we are. We are escaping from the prison of our own mind.

In this day and age, we have the opportunity to gain a remarkable amount of information. We keep an open mind. This is a chance – indeed it is our quest – to research these facts about our True Power in order to build the foundation for our great escape to freedom.

When traveling to a foreign country, we want to know about the tour guide? What are his qualifications? Does he know the terrain? Can he get me where I'm going? What does he want and need from me? Will he leave me stranded? Is he trustworthy? Does he get angered easily or is he calm, peaceful and caring? We are going somewhere far more important than just another country, so we research the Travel Guide.

Most people do not believe that they can define the type of True Power that they want and need. Most people were simply *told* what God is. That was the way it was. There was no mention of our True Power and we certainly didn't ask how it operates, much less how we can 'custom design' it. Well this is our chance.

When 'designing' our True Power, there are just a couple of restrictions. First, it must be benevolent and loving. Second, it must be a Power that has the ability to help us. Third, it operates by a set of universal laws.[19] As we develop a relationship with our True Power, we receive new information from it.

We sometimes wonder if we are truly capable of passing through this Gate. We might not feel equipped to define our True Power. Take heart. If we open our mind and express the willingness to work with it, it will work with us. We start to receive signs and guidance. We are

---

[19] Although we may not understand completely what those universal laws are, we attempt to make a start at understanding those laws and how our True Power operates. Our True Power may be able to work with much more powerful energies and with much more freedom than we operate which produces miracles. We may struggle to understand but it is still operating by universal laws and is therefore dependable. As we gain higher levels of understanding in time we refine our understanding of our self, our own power and the abilities and requirements of our True Power.

open to believing in a power that can aid us. Then we will start to see coincidences and even miracles.

In truth, miracles ought to take place frequently. When they don't, something is wrong. As we recognize coincidences and miracles, we know that we are on the right track. In truth, we are just removing the blocks to the awareness of the love that surrounds us. This, then, takes the form of miracles, which then become our way of life. Not only do we come to expect miracles, but we will begin to depend on them. Our trust in our True Power will increase and fear will begin to leave.

We do not let preconceived notions about spiritual terms prevent us from looking at this in a whole new way. At this point, it is important to lay aside judgment regarding organized religions. This is a matter of focus and desire. Everything and everyone has their perceived "good" and "bad" points. Judging organized religion is one of the first resentments that we need to let go of in order to progress on our spiritual Path. Indeed, researching religions and spiritual paths could be part of the research we do to find our True Power. Who knows what could be revealed.

We might have to revisit this Gate many times to shape and reshape our beliefs. What worked at one time in our life might not necessarily work at another time. After formally passing the 2nd Gate, many quickly go through Gates 1, 2 and 3 in their morning prayer by saying something like "I can't, but we can. So let's do it." Finally, in taking a productive look at the 2nd Gate of Trust, we are now ready to move forward to the Gate of Decision (decision to cooperate).

~~~~~~~~~~~~~~~~~~~~~~~~~~~~~~~~~~~~

God's message to me is "stay out of the way, but stay ready."- Anonymous

~~~~~~~~~~~~~~~~~~~~~~~~~~~~~~~~~~~~

Gate 3: Decision

We made a decision to cooperate with our True Power and consciously utilize the Universal Laws

The 3rd Gate is the Gate of Decision. Where the 2nd Gate requires that we either build a relationship with our True Power or we refine it, the 3rd Gate requires that we decide to cooperate with it. Its opposite is the Gate of Resistance. Our True Power cannot do anything for us without our consent. No matter how much it wants to, it cannot aid us, unless we are willing to accept help. There are seemingly exceptions, but this holds true, even if we *forget* to ask for help. So, instead of "turning our will over" to the care of our True Power, we decide to cooperate with it.

Bear in mind that we will not be giving permission to our True Power to help us, without the ability to take it back. In fact, it is very *easy* to take back control of our life. This is in a more or less destructive way that will cause pain for us or for others. That's one way to recognize we have taken our will back. Luckily, nothing goes to waste in God's economy. This is part of our learning process.

Our relationship with our True Power ideally mirrors the relationship of loving earthly parents. No doubt "offering our self" or "surrendering to" a True Power can feel very comforting, like being cradled in the lap of a loving parent. That's appropriate when we are spiritual babes, but not a necessarily as an adult. As a spiritually mature adult we may be called to take the mantle up for our True Power. This may be service work or it may be a situation which takes great courage. It takes the appropriate exertion of will. However, there are still times when we feel vulnerable and need our spiritual parent's comforting. But generally, there is a different relationship with parents as children grow up.

We are children of the Creator. So we are co-creators. As mature co-creators, we accept responsibility for our life and our work. Along with our True Power, we are ready to create miracles - not just for our self, but for others too.

That is a decision we make every day. Here's a little joke from 'the rooms.' Two frogs sat on a log. One frog decided to jump. How many were left on the log? Two. This joke commonly gets a round of giggles. It emphasizes the fact that, just because we make a decision, does not mean that we will take action on that decision. It means that we *plan* to take action.

For instance, on the advice of Glinda, Dorothy made the decision to visit the Wizard of Oz. Before she stepped onto the first brick of the yellow brick road to meet the Wizard, she passed through the 3rd Gate – the

Gate of Decision. In other words, Dorothy decided to cooperate with her True Power.

The original 3rd Step of AA states, "We made a decision to turn our will and our lives over to the care of God, as we understood Him." Many individuals believe in the idea of a power that exists outside of them. They might believe that this power exists up in Heaven. They might have been raised with this idea and it is comforting to them. However, it is equally correct if we perceive that our True Power exists within us – as a part of us. Hopefully, this question is already resolved this for us in the 2nd Gate.

In the 3rd Gate, the original phrase in the 3rd Step of AA, "we turned our will and our lives over," has been left out because, to many people, found the concept daunting. This is basically semantics, but we don't want anything to interfere with our budding spirituality. To some, it infers that there is a Power to which we must submit our whole being immediately. This concept of "submission" has connotations of a hostile takeover.

The concept of "surrender" has similar connotations, but with a subtle yet vast difference. The concept of surrender implies that we acted of our own choice. This is the true meaning of "turned our will and our lives over." This wouldn't be overwhelming if our will and our lives weren't the requirement. Some may not see this as correct, possible or attractive, especially initially. Thus the 3rd Step was modified into the current 3rd Gate, utilizing "the decision to cooperate" as the main philosophy. This retains the original spirit without the intimidating connotations.

That being said, our relationship with our True Power is derived by the depth of our trust in it and in our sincerity of decision to cooperate with it and the Universal Laws. Indeed, in its deepest forms, we are surrendering. However, if our view of God is one that is foreboding, it is frightening to surrender. Perfect surrender is not necessary to make a start. Any benevolent True Power does not want us to be frightened. It is worthy of our trust and is not offended if we question. It will not strike us down. Otherwise, many of us would have been "roasted" numerous times.

At some point, we surrender to our True Power because soothes our spirit. This happens as we grow in trust. We might liken our relationship with our True Power to the relationship of a martial arts master or guru. As we see results, our trust increases and we trust their guidance more and more. Later, this morphs into deep love.

This does not mean that we surrender our whole soul to a deity in blind faith - No. We must also make sure that we do not confuse the voice of our True Power with the voice of the ego. Discernment is key. We familiarize our self with how our True Power operates so that we can work together smoothly, as a team. If we mistrust its guidance at every turn, it slows down progress on our Path. We will become frustrated. There are times when we think that we are 'being taken for a ride.'

This happened to me in 2009. I followed the guidance of my True Power as closely. Subsequently, I lost my business and two homes, and then we were evicted. But had that *not* happened, I wouldn't have been witness to the awesome miracles that immediately followed. I started a more fitting career, acquired bigger and better properties, and co-founded a new business doing work that spoke to my heart. My family prospered as well. My husband and I are now able to help other people with food, housing and opportunities for recovery. I didn't suffer physically at all in the process but did struggle emotionally at times to understand my True Power. I learned so much and grew more fearless.

We have chosen a True Power. Now, our task is to cooperate with it. The more we cooperate with our True Power, the easier our life is. Ideally we don't block what our True Power is trying to accomplish by taking back our faith in it. That is like saying, "I don't like how this is going, so I am going to take control of this situation." This limits what our True Power can do. When we do this, we prevent it from manifesting miracles and it will seem as though it has led us down the wrong path. Then we become confused and disappointed.

Think of our True Power's plan like a plant. It needs to be planted, cultivated and cared for. It takes time to come to fruition. How long it takes depends on the type of plant. Let's say that we provide the water and our True Power provides what we cannot provide - the right amount of sunlight. One day, we decide that we don't like how the plant is looking, so we decide to dig it up. We remove it from the sunlight.

How do we think that's going to turn out? Not only did we pull up the plant and injure the roots. But, without sunlight, there's not much hope for its survival. We can continue to water it, but that will produce a muddy mess in the end. That's okay if we like mud. The moral of this story is: Don't pull up the plant before its fruition. Don't quit before the miracle happens.

On another point, if the idea of turning our will and life over to a True Power appeals to us, then we work with that idea. But we must be a clear channel in order to receive the guidance that our True Power offers us. The Rainbow Gates help us to become a clear channel. They are a conscious clearing and purification process.

We have chosen a True Power that is loving and benevolent. So it will always communicate helpful, loving thoughts and feelings to us. But, if we carry a lot of emotional negativity, it is our lower self[20] that we often connect with most easily. In contrast to the 'still small voice' of our True Power, that of our lower self is often loud or pushy. It can appear as the True Power at times. That's why great discernment is necessary at first, as well as the input of others.

No one can make contact with our True Power for us. It is our decision; no one else's. It is we who make the decision as to whether to trust our True Power. We declare our intention to cooperate with our True Power, listen; then act.

There are several prayers that are common in 12 Step programs. NA endorses a very simple 3rd Step prayer that reads like this: "Take my will and my life, guide me in my recovery and show me how to live."

In the original AA program, people once prayed, "God, I offer myself to Thee – to build with me and to do with me as thou wilt. Relieve me of the bondage of self that I may better do thy will. Take away my difficulties that victory over them may bear witness to those I would help of thy power, thy love, and thy way of life. May I do thy will always."[21]

However, we do not have to pray in this manner. We simply make contact consciously with our True Power. A benevolent True Power will always respect our boundaries. It never forces its will on us. That is the

---

[20] Negative ego - represented in Oz as the wicked witch.
[21] © *Alcoholics Anonymous*, Fourth Edition, page 63, reprinted with permission of Alcoholics Anonymous World Services, Inc.

reason it must be invited to help us during the day. Conversely, this is also the way to tell if a power is *not* benevolent.

Our True Power knows itself in relation to us. Similarly, we experience our self in relation to our True Power, as well as to all of Creation. Our will is as important to our True Power as its will is to us. Otherwise there is no co-creation.

It is best not to work through the Rainbow Gates alone but, rather, with a carefully chosen person. If this is done sincerely, we can experience a meaningful spiritual awakening.

Working through this Gate implies that we are making the decision to follow this Path, if it is the Path to which we are drawn. Any Path we walk requires us to cooperate with its conditions. If we have chosen this Path, we are making the choice in this 3rd Gate to follow through with the remaining Rainbow Gates. It is part of the decision to trust the universal laws by which we have decided to cooperate. If we do not follow through with our decision, we cannot accurately judge our True Power by the results obtained.

We greatly need our True Power to work for us, yet we often block the way through which it can work. Sometimes this is because we merely do not understand *how* to work with it. Other times, it is the obstinent ego that wants to prove that it is really alone and separate from any Power. That's one of the ego's main ideologies and the basis of the Nightmare of Nowhere.

The ego might say to us, "See, everything goes wrong for us and everyone is against us." Everyone has had this thought at least once in their life. This is referred to as the "victim mentality." It is part of the rebellious nature that initially started the Illusion.

Remember that, when the ego is thinking negatively, we will think negatively too - but only if we identify with it. We don't judge the ego or our self, not because it's "wrong" to judge, but because we are incapable of judgment. We sincerely ask our True Power for another perception – another way to see things.

We usually have many questions at this point. We might even have a great deal of fear. Don't worry, we are not expected to join a nunnery or monastery, and we probably will not be required to devote our life to missionary work, unless that is our heart's desire.

Our True Power knows our heart's desires better than we do because it put them there. It wants us to realize our dreams in a way that serves everyone's highest good. It gently guides us into a more beautiful way of life - one that moves at our pace. We are daily given many opportunities to learn. Everything flows as smoothly as we allow it to flow. But we need to be open to guidance.

The structured direction in these 12 Rainbow Gates will help us to get sure footing. Some say the word *God* stands for "Good Orderly Direction." The idea of "Great Organizing Dynamic" is Consciousness that organizes the functions of our body and every aspect of our lives. Think about it. Why does a house fall apart and start to deteriorate when no one is living in it? When a person's will to live is weak they will eventually develop diseases[22] because their mind is somewhere else - in the future of past. They want out of the pain. When a beloved passes on, the partner will soon follow because that is where their mind is – on the other side with the beloved. It is a very good reason mystics always speak of "being present." Meditation is focus on the now and ultimately organizes the life into flowing harmony.

As we pass through the Rainbow Gates, we walk our way out of the Nightmare by focusing on and harmonizing every aspect of our life. With time, we experience less and less fear, anger, depression, confusion, frustration, guilt, anxiety and self-pity. Time lets us progress at our own pace. We never complete our realizations because reality is ever expanding.

---

[22] Some research is showing that many cancer patients are ambivalent about living or had depression prior to the illness.

~~~~~~

"The unexamined life is not worth living."- Socrates

~~~~~~

Gate 4: Knowledge

We made a courageous and thorough personal and gratitude inventory.

The 4th Gate is the Gate of Self-Knowledge. This is quite different from the moral inventory that is used in AA[23].

The moral inventory works for many people, but not for this focus. The opposite of the Gate of Self-Knowledge is the Gate of Denial.

The 4th Gate is separated into two parts: a gratitude inventory and a personal inventory. The gratitude inventory is used to focus on our strengths, and all that is "right" with us, including our passions and purpose. The personal inventory covers all of the rest of the issues, from unwanted character traits (like fear and resentment) to those people toward whom we did not act lovingly. In this 4th Gate, the "moral inventory" in the original 4th Step of AA is replaced with "personal and gratitude inventory"[24] for neutrality reducing needless self-judgment.

In Oz, the scarecrow is a reflection of Dorothy's inner self; as is everything a reflection. After Dorothy meets him at the crossroads, he begins to reveal to her a personal inventory of a particular character trait that he feels he is lacking. He also reveals to her how he

---

[23] © *Alcoholics Anonymous,* Fourth Edition, pages 59, 64-71, reprinted with permission of Alcoholics Anonymous World Services, Inc.

[24] *Alcoholics Anonymous, actually uses the term "personal inventory" in the text.*

envisions himself if he can acquire that trait. Although the scarecrow's sharing of this is done at the 5th Gate, the self-inventory (which the scarecrow had plenty of time to perform while hanging on the post) exemplifies the passage through this 4th Gate.

Socrates, the Greek philosopher, once wrote, "An unexamined life is not worth living." There are a few ways in which this statement can be translated. When expressed in a constructive way, this famous idea means that our life must be examined if it is to be joyful. That is what the 4th Gate is all about.

This 4th Rainbow Gate is a fast route to the conscious awareness of our mind, heart and soul. It applies self-inquiry for spiritual evolution. There are many routes to enlightenment. Awareness is often mentioned in spiritual literature. Many people purify themselves by using types of physical, energetic, etheric or emotional purification. Those are powerful methods, but they are no substitute for the inner purification that a method like conscious self-inquiry can initiate. Neither is the Rainbow Gates a substitute for those other methods. But this process will make these other methods even more productive.

The 4th and 5th Gates are the first initiation into the spiritual world. But, before we pass through the 4th Gate, we must be sure that we have a solid foundation in the first three Gates. Passing through the 4th Gate might be the hardest thing we have done so far, or it might be quite simple for us. It depends on our perception. That's another irony.

This Gate is to be entered in the spirit of love because we will be reviewing the actions that we have committed, and then viewing those actions from the perspective of others who have been hurt. This doesn't mean that we should be condemning of our behavior but, rather, we will see from the perspective of how another might have felt. Remember that, although others can *feel* hurt, in reality, no harm can actually occur. ACIM purports that "Nothing real can be threatened. Nothing unreal exists. Herein lies the peace of God." This means that nothing we do can permanently harm anyone. Everyone is in charge of their own destiny.

On the other hand, people do not always feel that way and it is naturally helpful to acknowledge their perspective. Acknowledgment of their pain can be very loving. It can open us to the awareness of the love that surrounds us and that resides in us.[25] This is a courageous and humble perspective. What's the difference between pride and humility? Pride is about *who* is right; humility is about *what* is right.

The 4th Gate is separated into two parts: a gratitude inventory and a personal inventory. The

---

[25] Acknowledging other's pain is really part of the 8th and 9th Gate. We are simply taking inventory including others possible perspectives at this Gate.

gratitude inventory is a written list that focuses on our strengths (including our passion and purpose) and all that is "good" with us and the world. The personal inventory is a list that covers all of the rest of the issues, from our resentments and our fears, to unwanted character traits, to those people toward whom we did not act lovingly.

The original 4th Step of AA reads, "We made a fearless and thorough moral inventory of our self." In the 4th Gate, the word *moral* is omitted. To many people, this word implies severe judgment and is unhelpful to self-forgiveness which is a main concept of the Rainbow Gates.

Let's return to the idea of judging. Judgment is the labeling of something as "bad" or "good," or "better" or "worse." An objective look at behavior is warranted, but a judgmental look is not. Attempts at judgment should be avoided. Just decide if a thought or behavior is preferable. If we desire to be loving, then we prefer to exhibit helpful behavior versus unhelpful behavior. There is no "right" or "wrong." There are just preferences.

Many religions assert that inquiry of one's behavior is a Path to spiritual maturity. Inquiry is not judgmental. Nor is it subjective. It is objective. A pitfall here is becoming subjective and guilt-ridden over past behavior. Although some emotion is healthy, the point is to set we free, not further spiritual imprisonment.

We are objective as necessary to get the job done. We might imagine that we are a research investigator who is utilizing surveys. We are looking for the facts and evaluating them. We are trying to evaluate our behavior, how we live and what our habits are. We are uncovering what is in our subconscious that is blocking us from the life we want to live.

In the 4th Gate we are focused on how others have felt hurt in relation to our past behavior. For some of those people, we might think their feelings are *their* problem and that it has nothing to do with us. But, for now, try to perceive the situation from their point of view.

When we write our list, our behavior toward others will come to the surface of our conscious mind. Of course, we write down acts we've committed. But we must remember to also include acts of omission. For instance, negligence is an act of omission. Negligence is said to be more painful to children than punishment.

As we have discussed, we really cannot harm anyone in 'the illusion' because nothing happens in reality. Remember that it is an unreal 'state of mind'. However, although we cannot harm others, we might not have always *been helpful*. Essentially, we might have been unloving, or uncaring, or just distracted. That is what feels hurtful.

It is not the act that is important. It is the love or lack of it behind the act that is important. So now we have an opportunity to readdress our past behavior loving thereby healing it. We look at it as if we are being given another chance - because we are.

Working through this Gate will be very simple if we maintain objectivity. This does not mean being cold-hearted to others pain either. But easy does it. Work through it, but not without a trusted spiritual advisor. Maybe a therapist, priest, mentor or guru can offer their support. There are spiritual advisors or sponsors in Anonymous programs.

The Rainbow Gates website has more information for making these connections. Ideally, find someone for support who has written a personal inventory of their own in the past, or someone who has had rigorous spiritual or psychological training.

The 4th Gate requires that we ask our True Power for guidance and for the power to work through the Gate. We can make this personal inventory as lengthy or as short as we want, as long as it is thorough. Just sit down with a paper and pen, or at our computer. The more comprehensive it is, the more we awaken.

While we write, we can turn on some music; light some incense; sit at a coffee shop, etc. The point is to make the writing process as painless as possible. That does not mean that it must be comfortable or even that it *will* be. We might not be able to write alone. Maybe we will need to put our spiritual advisor or our trusted friend on speed dial. It is not easy- but it is worth it.

We keep our goal in the forefront of our mind. Remember that we are trying to escape from the Nightmare and get to the happy dream. We keep a balanced insight of the situations of which we are writing. We become the beholder. Viewing our self in an unloving manner will not help our passage through the Gates of Nowhere. We accept our self and our prior behavior, even if others do not.

We are beings of love. The closer we can come to this true vision of our self, the sooner we will get to the happy dream. Buddhists call this the Rainbow Bridge. It is the highest state that can be attained before attaining Nirvana. So, the closer we come to this true vision of our self, the closer we will be to Somewhere. This might be a tall order, but we make a start and put pen to paper. We try not to lose sleep.

The 4th Gate is simply about bringing into our consciousness the contradictions in our minds and hearts. These block our awareness of the love that surrounds us and that is who we are. The awareness of love in our life will feel like appreciation, abundance and joy. We feel the love and we delight in miraculous coincidences that happen regularly. Who doesn't want that?

When people start to work through the 4th Gate, they are often afraid that there is an overwhelming darkness that exists within them, which will overtake them. This fear can cause us to put off writing our personal inventory indefinitely. But this perception of fear is simply a lack of love.

The more judgmental we are of our self, the greater the fear. This is all the more reason to follow through with this Gate with emotional support on hand. We ask our self, "What is the worst that can happen?" What will we uncover that we are so judgmental of? The past needs to be fully exposed in the light of love. Then we can be free of it.

The written personal inventory is a powerful way to remedy denial. We don't simply talk our way through this Gate. In order for this Gate to be fully effective, we must complete a *written* inventory – if we can. We watch for temptations to either exaggerate or diminish our inventory to the best of our ability.

Self-centered fear is one of the most common items on these lists. Remember that this is the fear that we will lose something that we have or that we won't get something that we desire. Most, if not all, suffering comes from this alone.

We will also need to examine our resentments. Remember to include information regarding intimate relationships. This is usually the most potent area for secrecy. Don't leave any rock unturned.

It is just as important, if not *more* important, to take stock of our assets and everything we can be grateful for. This is tricky for some of us. But, even in the worst, there is goodness. We remember traits such as courage, honesty, kindness, or even skill sets that we have. This includes examining our passion and purpose in life. Certainly, there are many things that need to be addressed.

Gratitude is among the most important. It is proven that professionals who are in a positive mood are more productive. Doctors that are in a positive mood make 30 percent more correct diagnoses. In a clinical study of depression, the analysts found that the group who made weekly gratitude lists had significant improvements.[26] Developing an attitude of gratitude is so important that researchers are now claiming that it's one of the main keys to alleviating depression and improving our overall health. Along with taking an initial personal inventory, gratitude clears our minds and hearts of negativity.

We might not yet understand how this work can greatly affect our life and others. Be patient. When we are finished with the Rainbow Gates, we will be able to successfully engage in spiritually advanced practices. This Gate is intensive spiritual and emotional housecleaning. We trust and feel good about what we are

---

[26] Shawn Achor, TedX Talk, Happiness Advantage, Feb 25, 2014

doing. It is profound. This is the road less traveled. Even angels dare not tread here.

This is how we become honest with our self. Yet, do so lovingly, not in a self-demeaning way. How we see our self is how we see others and the world. This is worth repeating; how we see our self is how we see others and the world. We might not be completely successful in maintaining a nonjudgmental stance toward our self while we hold our self accountable. But we do our best. The next Gate will help us achieve more accurate self-perception.

Having done our best to pass through this 4th Gate, it is imperative for us to pass through the 5th Gate without delay. We are trying to put the past behind we – to let it go. This might seem impossible. But, with the help of our True Power and support from others, it is quite possible.

We must also have someone who supports us. Ask someone to hold we accountable on our spiritual journey in a loving way. Our willingness to ask for support is the key. Do we really want the reward of freedom and liberation? If so, then we are ready to move toward the outer Gates.

~~~~~~~~~~~~~~~~~~~~~~~~~~~~~~~~~~~~

"We can't save our face and our *** at the same time."- Anonymous

~~~~~~~~~~~~~~~~~~~~~~~~~~~~~~~~~~~~

Gate 5: Humbleness

We admitted to our self, True Power and another human being the exact nature of our blocks to the awareness of love.

The 5th Gate is called the Gate of Humbleness. It is very similar to the original 5th Step of the AA[27] program, which incorporates some Eastern philosophies. This Gate is not about humiliation. Nor is it about the theory of humility (which is often debated). Rather, it is about the practice of humbleness. If we can pass through this Gate, we either rejoin humanity or we deepen our link to humanity. To err is human. The opposite of the Gate of Humility is the Gate of Pride.

The phrase "We admitted... the exact nature of our wrongs" is removed from the original 5th Step of the AA[28] program and is replaced with "We admitted... the nature of our blocks to the awareness of love." This is one of the main concepts that are discussed in the 12 Rainbow Gates. Love cannot be taught; it can only be experienced. It is beyond words. However, the blocks to the awareness of love can be removed. When those blocks are removed, we will realize that love was there all along.

---

[27] © *Alcoholics Anonymous*, Fourth Edition, page 59,73-76, reprinted with permission of Alcoholics Anonymous World Services, Inc.

[28] © *Alcoholics Anonymous*, Fourth Edition, pages 59, 72 -78, reprinted with permission of Alcoholics Anonymous World Services, Inc.

We allow our True Power to do things for us by not blocking its power and its love for us. Then others will act lovingly toward us, like they never did before. Strangers will smile at us as we pass by. We will feel more compassionate and be truly helpful, without enabling others. Life will flow, good things will happen and we will ultimately get Somewhere. Not only will we get somewhere, but we will get somewhere that we truly want to go - without struggle. "We ceased fighting anything and anybody." Life becomes increasingly wondrous.

Dorothy and the scarecrow head down the yellow brick road where they encounter the tin woodsman. He has rusted all over and cannot move. But they fix him up by oiling him. The tin woodsman tells the group what he thinks he is lacking - his heart. In their opening interaction, the group has helped the tin woodsman pass through all of the Gates, right up to this 5th Gate. He felt powerless and unmanageable; he trusted that the wizard could help him; he decided to take action; he took a personal inventory; he told the others about it. Awesome.

We cannot pass through this 5th Gate alone. We must have those who are willing to go through with us and give us "oil" if we need it. Without someone compassionate to help us through this Gate, we may freeze up from the tears, unable to finish our journey.

Put another way, we need someone else to stand by with the oil can. We all need friends at times like these, especially for this work.

This Gate will let us take our first breath of freedom. There is still work to be done to *secure* our freedom, but we can see the exit at a distance. If we hold on to our secrets, it will be quite painful now. When we passed through the 4th Gate, we brought them into our consciousness. Now we must rid our self of them and be done with them.

Let us return to the idea of being helpful or unhelpful. What is real cannot be threatened. What is not real does not exist. The ego is not real. The body is not real. Therefore we cannot actually harm others. However, although we cannot harm others, we might not have always helped others either. Viewed another way, unhelpful is the same as unloving, uncaring, neglectful, etc. This is not merely semantics. There is a difference.

We can help someone anytime we act out of love because love is real and so is the spirit of the person being helped. Love reaches past the ego to the spirit. For instance, if we feed someone, it is not the food that is the helpful part - necessarily. The food is merely feeding the body, which is unreal. It is the love behind the act of feeding someone that is the helpful part in reality. In fact, in another situation, it might be more helpful *not* to feed someone. It's the love behind our decisions and actions that is meaningful and eternal.

Hopefully, these ideas will make it easier for us to tell our story. That's what it is – a story. It is our story of Nowhere and Nobody. If it is not serving us and others, it is something to let go of. In the future, our story will not be as painful for us as it is right now. Later, our story will be a source of strength to us, as well as to others who are still lost in Nowhere.

Many people forsake the Path at this point. Indeed, this can be a very difficult Gate to pass. It may seem very intimidating to tell someone about our secrets, behaviors, thoughts, obsessions, compulsions, resentments, attitudes and unwanted character traits.

Why should we do this? We may agree that it is probably important to admit these dark secrets to our self, but why should we have to share them with another? Isn't it enough that our True Power knows about them? Unfortunately, it is not. There is something deeply healing about seeing the face of another compassionate human being who knows our secrets. We will rid our self of the subconscious shame and isolation that separates us from others, from our True Power and from the awareness of love that surrounds us and that is us.

Of course, this person must be carefully chosen. They must understand and support us. They will perhaps be honored that we have chosen them. Sometimes, people visit another city or town to find this person. Some people see a priest who they know will keep their secrets. Some people choose a compassionate stranger whom they will never see again. We ask our True Power to help us find them.

Before we work through this Gate we might be concerned that no one will understand some of the things that we have done or the feelings that we have felt. We might fear rejection. This is where we truly experience the depth of the judgment that we hold of our self. We may even tremble and shake, or get nauseas. That's okay. We take a deep breath and ask our True Power to be with us and to give us strength. Remember, our goal is freedom. But, if we have done our homework and we have sought out the right person with whom to do this vital work, a miraculous healing will take place. Often, the person with whom we are sharing will tell us a similar story. This can be a time of healing for them too.

We will often find that we have looked upon our self far more harshly than anyone else has. We will see and feel what compassion, understanding and acceptance looks and feels like. We might cry. We might feel deeply ashamed and even be tempted to defend our actions and thoughts. But we will get through it. This is a vital Gate. It is a rare experience and another key to our freedom.

We might want to burn the paper upon which the personal inventory was written. On the other hand, we might need to keep it so that we can use it in the 8ᵗʰ and 9ᵗʰ Gates. In any case, this will be a sacred document. Treat it carefully so no one else will see it. It is also a sacred moment. It should be treated as such by us and by the other person. Saying a prayer to begin and end the experience creates a sacred space for this momentous event.

This Gate brings about true spiritual experience. If we do not destroy the inventory, treat it like it a priceless heirloom that we want to keep safe and private. This is for our protection and for those about whom we've written. It is a sacred responsibility.

Some people have experienced great illuminations at this time – even physically. When we walk through this Gate, at first we will likely be exhausted and will need rest. So we schedule time to care for our self afterwards. But then we will feel lighter and clearer. Indeed we are. Spirituality is no longer just a theory for us now. We are ready for the next level in our spiritual journey.

~~~~~~

I don't work the 6th Gate. It works me.

– MA LAXMI ANAND

~~~~~~

Gate 6: Willingness

We became ready to have these blocks to the awareness of love removed.

The 6th Gate is called the Gate of Willingness. This Gate requires that we become willing to have all of our character defects removed. But again, the 12 Rainbow Gates refer to these as "character traits," not as "character defects."[29] There's a major difference. Its opposite is the Gate of Reluctance.

Referring to something as a *trait* acknowledges that, at some point, it is useful in our lives. It may have saved our life or our sanity. This displays true gratitude for all aspects of our self and of others. In every moment, everyone and everything is exactly as it should be. However, it does acknowledge that a trait can, at present, block our awareness of the love that surrounds us. This is not a judgmental statement – it's a fact. Dorothy, the scarecrow and the tin woodsman encountered the witch leering from a rooftop. She threw a fireball at the scarecrow, and then warned him and the tin woodsman to abandon Dorothy. The group said that they had come a long way on their journey and that they were not going to turn back. With this affirmation, they

---

[29] © *Alcoholics Anonymous*, Fourth Edition, pages 59, 72, reprinted with permission of Alcoholics Anonymous World Services, Inc.

passed through the Gate of Willingness, and then set off into the dark forest.

Are we ready to have our True Power remove certain unwanted character traits from us? Do we want to progress along our spiritual Path? Then this Gate will serve in aligning our will with the will of our True Power.

The original 6th Step of AA reads, "We became willing to have these defects of character removed." By modifying this phrase, judgment is removed because it is called a "block to the awareness of love" instead of "defects of character."[30] Notice that the word *defect* is no longer used. Part of the reason for this is that "the defect" might have saved our life at one point. But now it is no longer useful or helpful, or it causes chaos to some degree. So we want it removed. That's all – no need for judgment.

As we pass through the 6th Gate, pay attention to the character traits that are still causing pain for us or for others. Pain should not be equated with harm. Pain is simply the touchstone that something needs to change.

Most likely, our unwanted character traits will not all be removed at once. I'm sure that there are exceptions to this, such as Christ or Gandhi. However, even after the Buddha became enlightened, he held several character traits that would be considered

---

[30] © *Alcoholics Anonymous*, Fourth Edition, page 59, reprinted with permission of Alcoholics Anonymous World Services, Inc.

misogynistic by today's standards because women were not originally allowed in the monastic Order. But some character traits are easier to let go of than others. They begin quietly at first, and then they begin to declare themselves.

Some years ago, my husband was suffering from an infection that was caused by a tooth. Despite his complaints of being in pain, the dentist felt that, if it was really something that needed to be addressed, it would "declare itself." Then he went on his way to a Saturday morning game of golf.

It was an agonizing weekend for my husband. By Monday, the infection had loudly declared itself. This may be an extreme example. But the point is that we don't have to dig for unwanted character traits. We will know what to work on because the character trait will declare itself. It will let us know that it's time to let it go. It will become increasingly painful to keep. That's the beauty of the 6th Gate.

Here's another example... When people go into recovery, they often need to gain weight. So they consume as much food as they want. That's great but, later, they find that they have gained more weight. Now, they may begin to experience an increasing amount of pain in their knees. If they continue in the same manner, they begin to experience other issues, such as high cholesterol and heart palpitations. The problem is declaring itself louder and louder. Ideally, we hear the declaration sooner, rather than later. This is just one example of how the 6th Gate can "work us." But everyone's level of pain tolerance is different. This is not a moral issue; it is more of a personal preference.

It might be harder to remove unwanted character traits that are hidden, such as false pride, greed, fear, anxiety or depression. The 4th and 5th Gates will have planted the seeds in our consciousness of traits that we need to pay attention to. We will notice blocks to the presence of love as they declare themselves. In other words, as these traits become more painful, we will desire relief from them. It becomes a natural process.

Before we passed through the Rainbow Gates, we might have been able to indulge in these habits with little repercussion. But now, we have become conscious of them. Having grown very rapidly by passing through the Rainbow Gates, we find that some of these traits must be dealt with immediately. They seem to be far more painful.

The less painful traits can and will wait. It is most likely that they will remain if we do not make a conscious decision for them to leave. When it comes time, we will want them to leave due to increasing discomfort. Still other traits will need to be removed as we advance spiritually. Ironically, when we pray to become willing to have these character traits removed, we may find that they actually become even *more* uncomfortable for us. We don't let this deter us from asking for willingness.

On the other hand, our True Power can use us for good, even with our blocks and unwanted character traits intact. Nothing goes to waste in the Universal economy. If we find that, with repeated attempts, we simply cannot release, or let go of, a painful trait or habit, move on to the 7th Gate. Try not to become anxious or feel defeated. We will simply feed the ego's idea that "we are not good enough" and energize that block. This is but a small bump in our Path. We are making great headway toward freedom. Having endured this Gate, we are now prepared to ask our True Power for its gifts in the 7th Gate.

"If we're going to pray for potatoes, we'd better grab a hoe"-Irish quote

Gate 7: Purification

We sincerely asked our True Power to remove the blocks to the awareness of love, seeing our self as our True Power sees us.

The 7th Gate is the Gate of Purification. It points out that part of the process of actually removing an unwanted character trait requires that we envision our own perfection. Its opposite is the Gate of Contamination.

Remember how the scarecrow, tin man and lion envisioned themselves when they attained knowledge, heart and courage? This is the process. What superb examples. We still have to ask for the help of our True Power in the removal of a trait, but there is a distinct difference in how that takes place.

The phrase "humbly" was removed from the original AA 7th step[31] and "sincerely" was inserted to *more adequately* reflect the proper spirit in modern language. Our unwanted character traits are eased by our desire for perfection. However, progress not perfection is our motto. We are the children of the Universe and we are quite perfect, even though it might not feel like it right now. This is the perception that our True Power already holds of us - perfection. We are not what we do. We are not even our personality. We are far more than that.

However, this does not mean that there isn't work for us to do. If there are things that we can and must do, we cannot expect our True Power to do them for us. For instance, if we want to reduce our consumption of <u>chocolate ice cream, don</u>'t buy it, and then, after eating

[31] © *Alcoholics Anonymous*, Fourth Edition, page 59, reprinted with permission of Alcoholics Anonymous World Services, Inc.

most of it, claim that we bought it for the kids. No judgment - but certainly, when we have done our part, we can expect miracles. Millions have experienced them. It works when we work it.

The journey to Oz, which was undertaken by our friends, involves finding the wizard and asking him for help. Each and every time that Dorothy and her friends sing songs or reminisce about what they desire, they pass through the 7th Gate. Do we notice how pleased they look while they sing songs? They are masters of visualization. Maybe we should all make up songs about what our life will be like when the blocks to love are removed.

In the 6th Gate we released the unwanted character traits that we could release by our own efforts. We did what we reasonably could. This does not mean we drive our self to insanity. That would defeat the point, wouldn't it? Perhaps those blocks were not much of a problem. Maybe it was mainly a matter of increasing our awareness of them. However, for other, more stubborn, character traits, we may need help from our True Power.

If we can *easily* handle something our self, empowered by regular prayer of course, why would we leave it to our True Power to handle for we in the 7th Gate? Well, there are situations for which we will need our True Power to act on our behalf. If we could have taken care of this by our self we would have done so at this point in the Rainbow Gates and in our life. This situation is unique for everyone. If we believe that we have a problem, which we have repeatedly tried to conquer by our own power, but we do not seem to be making progress with it, it is appropriate to ask for help from our True Power. How great is that.

By the time we arrive at this 7th Gate we will have developed a solid relationship with our True Power. Now we are able to turn to this great Power and ask it for something extraordinary – a miracle. A miracle is something that our True Power can do for us (and often through us), but that we cannot do for our self.

Some people have a problem asking for help. But that is simply a matter of ego. Again, it's worth repeating, if we could have taken care of this by our self then we would have done so at this point in the Rainbow Gates and in our life. That doesn't mean that we should stop trying. It means that we cease struggling and try something different. There is a subtle, but key, difference. We surrender here. How this looks in each situation is different.

Ask our True Power to give us the power we need in order to accomplish our task. Our True Power will be glad to help. Some people have experienced dramatic and immediate relief of the removal of unwanted character traits simply by going through the 6th Gate. But the removal of some traits require extra Power from the 7th Gate. Look at it this way...

We are walking along a Path that has stones all along it. We easily throw most of them off the Path and, when we can see bigger stones, we say a quick 7th Gate prayer and find the extra power to push them off of our path. We begin to feel pleased with our self, our True Power and life.

But then we come across a big boulder that is embedded in the dirt. In fact, it's huge. We push and push, but the boulder will not budge. We cannot go any further on our path because the rock is blocking our path. As a matter of fact, this boulder might flatten us with one wrong move. We decide to stop, sit down and sincerely ask our True Power for help in the 7th Gate. Our True Power might guide us to dig around it, and then it tells us how to leverage it with a log and a stone. We find amazing strength that couldn't possibly be ours alone and the boulder moves. It was not as hard as we thought it would be. We are amazed at our self and at our True Power. This is how our True Power can and will work for us.

Since this might be the first time we have asked for a character trait to be removed, it might require great faith on our part. Believe that our True Power sincerely wants to help us and that we are important to it – very important. Our True Power is never too busy for us.

There is no one who is more important to our True Power than us.

Keep in mind that, although our willingness to have a character trait removed is all that is required for spiritual advancement, sometimes it is not in our best interest. Or it could be that we are not ready for it to be removed. For instance, if we are a workaholic, that trait might be helping us provide for our family at this time.

Our unwanted character traits will disappear when our True Power doesn't need us to hold onto them anymore. Sometimes self-acceptance or humility is a larger, more important lesson. Trust our True Power, even if it does not remove all of our unwanted traits at once. There is always a reason for everything that happens. Everything is working for our good.

Initially, I possessed character traits, such as stubbornness and rigidity, which my True Power would not remove. But, had they not been there, I would not have accomplished some of the major things in my life for which those traits were needed. Once I achieved certain things, such as a Master's degree and the founding of a nonprofit corporation, my True Power let me know that they were no longer necessary and that they needed to be moderated. Awesome. I was ready for some fun and relaxation.

For as long as I have known, there have been disagreements about this Gate in regards to who is responsible for what. Some people believe that, if we want to rid our self of an unwanted character trait, we just have to keep working on our self. The other viewpoint is that, if we could do it our self, we would have. But there is a third perspective, which is exemplified by these two phrases, "If we're going to pray for potatoes, we'd better grab a hoe," and "God will do for us what we cannot do for our self."

When we are working through this Gate, an attitude of humility is best. We might want to perform a sacred ceremony, or get down on bent knees and ask for help. Just ask with sincerity and with the belief that our True Power has the best of intentions for us. We can work through this Gate daily. It certainly won't hurt to do so. Thank our True Power for the gifts that we desire. If we want fear removed, thank our True Power for fearlessness and courage. I prefer fearlessness. However, perfect love covers it all.

When we prepare our self to the best of our ability in the Gate of purification, we are ready for the 8th Gate – the Gate of Thoughtfulness. We are almost to the outside Gates. Smell the brisk air of freedom.

~~~~~~~~~~~~~~~~~~~~~~~~~~~~~~~~~

"It is better to understand than to be understood."-
Saint Francis of Assisi

~~~~~~~~~~~~~~~~~~~~~~~~~~~~~~~~~

Gate 8: Thoughtfulness

We made a list of all persons, including our self, that we acted unloving toward and became willing to make amends with them all.

The 8th Gate eight is called the Gate of Thoughtfulness. This Gate requires that we become willing to make amends to our self and to those whom we have not acted lovingly toward. It uses the phrase "those we acted unlovingly toward" in place of "those we had harmed."[32] Its opposite is the Gate of Thoughtlessness.

We might ask, "If I have not harmed anyone, why do I need to make amends?" The 12 Rainbow Gates teach us that Nowhere is an illusion in which nobody is harmed. Only love is real. Only love and loving acts have an impact in reality. So, in reality, nobody is harmed. However, their experience in Nowhere creates a false *belief* that they can be harmed. Although it is a false belief, it is a real experience.

If people can accept the gift that is offered in a "harmful" situation, it gives them something precious and eternal. They are healed; demonstrating that they are not harmed which is a permanent state. For instance, when a person chooses to truly forgive, they experience more clarity, love and universal understanding, which support their decision to forgive. But this gift is accepted after

[32] © *Alcoholics Anonymous*, Fourth Edition, page 59, reprinted with permission of Alcoholics Anonymous World Services, Inc.

the decision to forgive, not before. In any difficult or traumatic situation, there is a gift of enlightenment, however small that may be. But, how can anything eternal be small? Since harm is unreal, the eternal gift is always greater than the harm that has been done. As people redeem the gift of love in its myriad of forms, they are released from the illusion.

Some people don't know how to do this. Others would simply rather keep their resentments. In either case, they might need our help; they might need our amends. In our amends, which is a type of miracle, could erase any symptoms of their perceived harm, revealing that no permanent damage has been done. Not only will we be helping them, but we will be helping our self as well. We are our brother's keeper because our brother *is* us.

Healing often transpires during acts of love. Acts of love are thoughtful by nature. When the Gate of Thoughtfulness is properly executed, there is a powerful healing that can take place in both parties when making amends. Proper thoughtfulness for amending relationships ensures the best outcome for all parties concerned.

Dorothy, the scarecrow and the tin woodsman meet the cowardly lion. The cowardly lion represents fear and the need for courage. When he tries to intimidate Dorothy's little dog, Toto, she slaps his face. Although the lion's behavior is akin to someone hurting an innocent creature, if we want to make amends, we have to focus on how we behaved toward someone, despite their abuse. Hopefully, we will have worked this out in the 4th and 5th Gates.

Dorothy's behavior here was in protecting an innocent creature. She has nothing to apologize for. Some people might feel "bad" for protecting themselves or others. We do have a right to protect our self, but some people have the value of passivism. These are values we must decide for our self. For instance, for those who have passivism as a value and don't believe in defending the body, (e.g., Ghandi, Martin Luther King, etc.), self-defense would be a unwanted character trait.

Now, back to our story... The group holds a discussion about whether to invite the cowardly lion on their journey to see the wizard. This is an act of thoughtfulness on their part. Also, the moment before the stunned lion made amends was an example of an awkward pass through the 8th Gate. Nonetheless, the group has passed through the 8th Gate together.

The philosophy of ACIM infers that no one can, in fact, harm another. But most people truly believe that, if we have done something to someone to cause them to feel pain, we have harmed them.

If we passed the 4th Gate with this in mind, we will be able to make a list of those people who believe that we have harmed them. Keep in mind that, from their perspective, we *have* harmed them. However, definitely do not debate with them the definition of the word *harm*. We rehearse what we will say to them so that we can acknowledge their feelings, and then give them our full attention. Commit to memory that this is the Gate of Thoughtfulness - not the Gate of Debate.

The original 8th Step of AA reads, "We made a list of all persons we had harmed and became willing to make amends to them all." Although intellectually, we might believe in the philosophy of ACIM or in another spiritual philosophy, there is no substitute for the act of making amends with another human being. This is similar to the 5th Gate in which we told another human being about our unwanted character traits. In a real sense, we were receiving forgiveness.

The act of forgiveness is potent healing for our soul. However, in this 8th Gate we are still just making a list of those individuals to whom we need to make amends, and then thoughtfully planning the event. So, in this Gate, all we want to do is to be *willing* to make amends. We will also start to make a plan as to how we will *go about* making amends. This is similar to the 4th and 6th Gates in that we are performing an act of willingness. Actually, Gates 2, 4, 6, 8, 10 and 12 are Gates of willingness that prepare us for action.

This does not necessarily make it easy for us. But it should make the amends process *easier* by breaking it down into phases. We must be honest about our relationships. We can look back at the 4th Gate for guidance if we saved the work. It is better to understand than to be understood. In other words, don't try to make the people on our list understand our side. Just try to understand theirs. Help them to feel that they have been heard so that they can release their pain. We resist the urge to justify what we did.

In talking about making amends, we will find that it is truly more important that these people finally feel that they are being heard, understood and recompensed by us. We might not always agree with their perspective of the events that surround their pain. However, we are willing to make a reasonable thoughtful effort to amend the relationship.

We might practice mirroring back what we think they will say about our behavior. In psychological circles, this is called "reflective listening." Practice with a spiritual advisor or friend. It is a vital element in communication. When someone tells us how hurt or angry they feel, simply mirror back what they said, but from their perspective.

This does not mean that we are agreeing with what they said. If Mary told us that she felt hurt when we didn't pay her back the money we owe her, we might remember that we had a disagreement and that we do not owe her anything. In our amends to her, we would mirror her perspective as closely as possible. We might say, "I'm sorry that you felt hurt when I didn't return the money to you. I think there is a misunderstanding. How can we resolve this?" We may feel that we just want to amend the relationship, but are not necessarily willing or able to give her the money she feels that she is entitled too. Sometimes, there are no easy answers. Each situation takes some forethought. For this reason, it is strongly suggested to work through this Gate meditatively and with an objective party.

As in the previous example, sometimes it is also equally important not to take responsibility for something if it will not be helpful to do so, or if it is not the truth. But truth is subjective. For example, it is fairly common for an abused spouse to feel responsible for the abuse. Although this is clearly not the truth, it does happen. Hopefully, if we had these issues, we worked them out when we passed through the 5th Gate with a wise partner. If not, the 8th Gate is a great place to begin to carefully think about how, when and where we should make amends. Sometimes trying to make amends to an unloving person might actually instigate more acting out or abuse. We must think these situations out prayerfully and thoughtfully. That is another reason why this Gate is called the Gate of Thoughtfulness.

Sometimes the opposite is true and we think that *we* are the victim but, in fact, it is we who were acting unlovingly. In other words, we were projecting. Take responsibility and bear in mind that, when we engage in unloving behavior, we also harm our self. We are not an island either. We always have an effect on others.

The high ideal to which we hold our self is that we act lovingly. Anything unloving is not helpful. It may not be harmful, but it's not helpful either. On the other hand, we are only responsible for keeping our side of the "street" clean. It will do us no good to judge the people that are on our amends list. This will only pull our spiritual advancement backwards.

As we advance spiritually, our more subtle unhelpful behavior toward others may start leaping into our conscious mind. We will become increasingly sensitive to our own unloving behavior.

While planning our amends, we may discover that people have passed on, or we might find that we cannot locate them or, perhaps, we didn't even *know* them. Perhaps the person is still smarting from the incident in the past. They might not understand that we have changed our view of the situation and would like to make amends. They might feel so insulted by us that our mere presence would be very upsetting to them. If this is the case, ask our self and our True Power if we are helping them by making amends directly.

In some of these situations, we may plan to make "living amends." For instance, we might make a donation to an organization, or volunteer our time, at a place that is/was important to that person. We volunteer for a cause that *they* supported.

If the person is deceased, we might write a letter, and then visit their grave to make amends. We must make amends as sincerely as we can. This is more powerful than we might think. For example, many people begin to cry when they visit a grandparent's grave. I did. Every time it has been so beautiful and healing. So we make a sincere effort to locate those people to whom we need to make amends. Using the Internet, we can locate almost anyone.

I just located someone after 27 long years and was able to make amends. He said, "I'm really sorry if we have been carrying any kind of burden all these years, but please let it go. I have no hard feelings at all and remember you very fondly." I cried and felt the impact for three days. I was freer. I didn't realize how constraining it had been for me to not make that amends. It was a burden that I had held in my subconscious for nearly three decades.

It is important not to confuse the 8th Gate with the 9th Gate. The 8th Gate is not about *making* amends; it is about the *willingness* to make amends and about the *planning* of it. Making amends are sacred events and this is the planning stage for all of those events.

This Gate brings to life the details of the amends to be made. Each detail must be carefully thought out. We should have somebody whom we trust assist we with our passage through this Gate. At the very least, we must have somebody to offer advice if we get stuck.

At this point, we might be bristling with excitement, but also with worry. We have a new understanding of what unloving actions are and we have planned our release to freedom. Not to worry. We are near the last checkpoints.

~~~~~~~~~~~~~~~~~~~~~~~~~~~~~~

"People do not attract that which they want, but that which they are"-James Allen

~~~~~~~~~~~~~~~~~~~~~~~~~~~~~~

Gate 9: Love

We made direct amends to such people wherever possible and when helpful.

The 9th Gate is called the Gate of Love. Its opposite is the Gate of Fear. Here, love is concerning the act of mending broken relationships with others, as well as with oneself.　It expands upon the idea of amends, thoughtfulness and helpfulness.　The expression "except when to do so would injure them or others," is removed from the original 9th Step of the AA[33] program and is replaced with "when helpful."

This Gate can be infused with miracles, but also with snares.　While the next Gates are for remaining in the happy dream, the 9th Gate is the last Gate we must work through in order to leave the Nightmare of Nowhere altogether.

For example, despite his abuse, the group acted out of love toward the lion.　But this took place only after he admitted that he was a coward, and then apologized. He admitted he was mistaken. Admission of 'wrongdoing' is an act of love. The lion wanted to change and took action to make amends.　The Oz group made an ally out of an enemy.　At that point, they passed through the 9th Gate together.

---

[33] © *Alcoholics Anonymous,* Fourth Edition, page 59, reprinted with permission of Alcoholics Anonymous World Services, Inc.

It is true that we cannot harm others, but we can be less than helpful. Whether we are "right" or "wrong," when we are not helpful, people usually believe and react as though they have been harmed. So we should approach the people on our list with patience, compassion, sincerity and humility, if indeed they should be approached at all. It is better to work through the 9th Gate with our carefully chosen person for emotional support and in case any problems come up.

There are certain situations in which making direct amends are not helpful and can even be dangerous. However, direct amends are the ideal and a very powerful part of our spiritual journey. There is no experience like it.

We just need to keep in mind that, when amends are made without planning or, when they are made prematurely, they usually do not turn out well for either party. They might have been thought out in haste or in poor timing. Regarding our attitude toward those on our list, it should not be self-satisfied. Amends must be made humbly.

Remember that these humans are not mere means to an end. If we treat them simply as "stepping stones," they will know it. So we must try to be sensitive to their needs. They may still hurt from the incident that took place in the past. They might not understand that we have changed. If they are extremely agitated as we approach them, we must ask our self if we are truly helping them by making amends directly. Certainly, we procure their permission to approach them at all. Just be sensitive.

Most people will forgive others when they realize that their suffering was not in vain. For instance, Jane tolerates Jack's "bad" habits of drinking and brawling. When Jack changes his behavior, Jane is healed too because she was sharing Jack's spiritual journey. So people are often validated when we make amends. Most people are this way; some are not.

Some people believe that it is not our business what others think of us. This is true if we cannot reasonably do anything about it. However, if we believe that human beings are all connected, then would it not be to our advantage to amend those relationships that can be amended? The 9th Gate is the opportunity to do just that.

Let's look at the word *amend*. The Merriam-Webster dictionary defines it as "to change or improve" something. How could there be anything "wrong" with changing a "bad" relationship to a "good" one, or even simply improving upon it? We are not taking responsibility for situations that are not our responsibility. Nor are we required to make peace with an abusive dictator. But there is a way to see someone's viewpoint without necessarily agreeing with it. Often, that's all people want and need in order to amend a relationship – to feel understood. But often, they need to know that we have changed too – or at least that we are *trying* to change.

Try not to procrastinate, or be prideful or judgmental. This will bring everything to a screeching halt. Remember that we are not responsible for anyone else's behavior. We must focus on our journey and on our well-deserved freedom, instead. Our resentment is our business because resentment is like poison that we drink in the hopes that someone else will suffer.

When we actually start making amends, we might feel fearful. We might even tremble. This is common. This is the test that every spiritual warrior must pass. Remember that we want to free our self of guilt. Guilt and shame are thieves of joy.

The 9th Gate releases *us*. We are the main benefactor. Amends is not beneficial for the other party, unless they take advantage of it and forgive us. We have no power over whether they forgive us or not. But we will certainly advance in our spiritual awakening. On the other hand, be prepared to accept the reactions of the persons on our list. Be prepared for anything - from complete loving forgiveness to absolute disgust.

Always play it safe. If it is not safe to be with someone alone, meet them in public. It is our task to make amends, but not at the risk of injury or even emotional abuse. Similarly, it is not our responsibility to try to convince others that we deserve their forgiveness. This is very important. Do not make their forgiveness or understanding a requirement of our amends. Like the Gate of Thoughtfulness, this is the Gate of Love, not the Gate of Debate. Simply move on.

Spontaneous opportunities for amends do occur. So be prepared. Timing is very important. We might just find that an appropriate opportunity unexpectedly presents itself to us. So be ready to recall our well-thought-out plan from the 8th Gate.

In the 8th Gate, we worked out the details of how we are going to make amends. This should have prepared us for the opportunity to do so. If the person coincidentally shows up in our life, we can assume that it is a divinely inspired meeting. This happens a lot. However, if there is reason that the situation is inappropriate, let the opportunity pass. If the opportunity never presents itself again or, if we decide that it is best not to make direct amends, we can make a "living amends."

In legal matters, it is recommended that we follow the advice of our attorney, especially if there is a possibility that it could affect our family or our business associates. The 9th Gate does not require that we martyr our self, or that we involve our self or others in abusive or dangerous situations. However, most often, miracles can and do happen. Many people are reunited with family, relationships are healed, friendships are mended, financial records are cleared, resentments are banished and misunderstandings are forgiven. This is where the promises come true:

If we are painstaking about this phase of our development, we will be amazed before we are halfway through. We are going to know a new freedom and a new happiness. We will not regret the past nor wish to shut the door on it. We will comprehend the word serenity and we will know peace. No matter how far down the scale we have gone, we will see how our experience can benefit others. That feeling of uselessness and self-pity will disappear. We will lose interest in selfish things and gain interest in our fellows. Self-seeking will slip away. Our whole attitude and outlook on life will change. Fear of people and economic insecurity will leave us. We will intuitively know how to handle situations which used to baffle us. We will suddenly realize that God is doing for us what we could not do for ourselves. Are these extravagant promises? We think not. They are being fulfilled among us - sometimes quickly, sometimes slowly. They will always materialize if we work for them.[34]

Working through the 9th Gate improves the feeling of connectedness with other human beings. This Gate will help us to clear any guilt that we hold and any anger that is held toward us. Unconditional love will renew our belief that a wonderful life is possible. Great courage and faith are now rewarded with the keys to our freedom.

---

[34] © *Alcoholics Anonymous*, Fourth Edition, page 83, reprinted with permission of Alcoholics Anonymous World Services, Inc.

In order to maintain our freedom, we will need to incorporate the next three Gates into our daily life. Now we proceed to the Gate of Awareness. After this gate we are no longer bound to stay in the Nightmare of Nowhere. We can travel wherever we like, without fear.

~~~~~~~~~~~~~~~~~~~~~~~~~~~~~

When we can look with gratitude at the things that we think hold us back, a whole new joy descends upon us

– MA LAXMI ANAND

~~~~~~~~~~~~~~~~~~~~~~~~~~~~~

Gate 10: Awareness

We continued to take a daily gratitude and personal inventory and when we were unloving promptly admitted it.

The 10th Gate is the Gate of Awareness. It is one of the three Maintenance Gates. It maintains the happy dream. Its opposite is the Gate of Complacency. In the 10th Gate, a mini-gratitude inventory, which mirrors the inventory in the 4th Gate, is added to a daily personal inventory. For many people who are in recovery, this Gate eventually becomes a way of thinking, "Do I need to make amends for that? Where am I going? Today, I am grateful for..."

The act of making amends was retained from the 10th Step of the AA program, but the phrase, "when we were wrong,"[35] was replaced with "when we were unloving." This frees us from judging our self and frees us from the belief that we must behave perfectly at all times. We are already perfect. To err is human, but to make amends is saintly.

There is an interesting psychological phenomenon that exists in humans, which is that, when we do not behave lovingly, it is as if we do not love our self. In other words, we cannot do something to others without doing it to our self. Our mind knows no difference.

[35] © *Alcoholics Anonymous*, Fourth Edition, page 59, reprinted with permission of Alcoholics Anonymous World Services, Inc.

"Right" or "wrong," most people believe that our actions affect them. If our actions are less than loving, then we have already been unloving to our self. We might actually be hurting from our own assault on someone else. In both of these situations amends will be helpful. Make amends quickly to keep our spiritual channels clear. We don't want to spend one moment more than needed in the Nightmare of Nowhere.

Isn't it great that we have a world, which will reflect back to us our own thoughts so that we can become conscious of them and treat *our self* better? No matter what happens, we always hurt our self before we hurt others.

Now, let's define the difference between the words *hurt* and *harm*. Harm is the perceived permanent loss of something, (e.g., innocence, joy, time, love etc.). It implies that someone did something "wrong" that cannot be made "right." We have lost something and that often brings about feelings of vengefulness or depression. However, remember that we can accept a miracle that heals the situation. So harm is an illusion.

Hurt is perceived as a painful, but temporary, experience. If we perceive hurt, correctly, as being unreal, it will disappear as we apply spiritual principles, such as forgiveness and love. This is one reason that amends can be so powerful. They are miracles of love.

Amends deliver miracles that free both us and our brother or sister. Miracles are delivered by love.

As Dorothy's family of five came out of the dark forest and saw Emerald City, they were enthralled. They ran toward the Gates of the city, but became overwhelmed by sleep when they ran through a poisoned poppy field.

This Gate represents our growing awareness and the ongoing commitment to that awareness. Put another way, it is the commitment to awaken from the dream. This is the challenge of this part of the journey – awareness. We have come out of the dark forest, but if awareness slips away, we could fall back to sleep.

As was previously mentioned in the 4th Gate, developing an attitude of gratitude is so important that researchers claim that it can be one major solution to alleviating depression and improving our overall health. Likewise, taking a personal inventory and making amends will keep our mind and heart clear.

It is so important to keep the progress we have gained and to continually move forward. As it is in physics, we are either moving forward or backward; we are never standing still. Also, objects in motion tend to stay in motion. We want to keep ours in an "upward" trajectory. We have already discovered that, in order to get Somewhere, we need to incorporate gratitude, prayer, meditation and service work into our life. But, sometimes, we might unconsciously test our self to see how long we can ignore those disciplines. That is part of spiritual training.

We might think, "Oh, I don't have time to meditate, I have this test to study for." We struggle through the test. But, next time, we choose to meditate and find that the meditation increases our capacity to retain information, so we pass the test with flying colors. Not only that, but we feel calmer and more confident. We just wish that we had put meditation on a higher priority list earlier. That's part of learning.

The contrast will let us know when we are slipping backwards. We may find that we are irritable or snappy with people. Just call upon our True Power. With the help of our True Power, we will be back on the Path and all will be well again.

This process results in learning about our spiritual needs. After we have formally completed these Gates, the 10th Gate may be the only one that we write out on a daily basis. Still later, it might become part of a mental routine of self-inquiry. Many people in recovery say that this is the case for them. They simply ask themselves at the end of the day if they feel good about how they treated others throughout the day and whether they made amends as necessary. Still others journal daily.

The 4th and 10th Steps in the original 12 Steps of AA do not contain a gratitude inventory.[36] But the 4th and

10th Gates do. Our True Power doesn't need our gratitude, but we do. There is great power in making a gratitude inventory. Ideally, we should acknowledge our gratefulness for at least three different things in our life every day. This will affect our attitude tremendously.

The 10th Gate is a miniature version of the 4th Gate. If we continue to take daily inventory and, if we are very persistent with it, we might never have to pass through the 4th Gate again. Nonetheless, we will still need someone in which we can confide regularly. It is important that everyone has someone whom they trust and who they can talk to about their spiritual issues. The AA program recommends that members have a spiritual advisor or sponsor but this is not found in the book specifically.

Basically, continuing to take personal inventory means that we make a habit of inquiry of our self, the situations in our life, values, ethical issues, behaviors, thoughts, attitudes and beliefs. Also, we decide if we are truly following our passions and our purpose for our life - everyday. Are we moving forward on our Path? Otherwise, old ways of thinking and behaving will return. Spiritual growth requires continual effort. This is a discipline. We are either going Somewhere or we are heading Nowhere.

---

[36] © *Alcoholics Anonymous*, Fourth Edition, page 59, reprinted with permission of Alcoholics Anonymous World Services, Inc.

If we want to remain on the Path and be a clear channel for the guidance of our True Power, promptly admit whenever we do not behave lovingly. This is vital. There is no reason to let guilt weigh on our shoulders. We want to stay in the happy dream. Just make amends. It's that simple. Otherwise, we might find our self living in the Nightmare again.

It might be helpful to make a customized daily inventory that we can quickly fill out at the end of the day. To determine which unwanted traits regularly cause we pain, we can refer to the work we completed when we passed through the 4th and 6th Gate writings. We know what they are.

Make several copies of our inventories, and then put them in a folder and set the folder beside our bed. Glance briefly at the list of our unwanted traits, and then quickly affirm the opposite trait – those that we want to affirm. Be sure to thank our True Power for helping us to do what we could not do for our self.

Practice acceptance of our thoughts and behaviors. This is easier if we accept our self as a human being. Remember that to err is human. Human beings do make mistakes. But really there are no mistakes. Just examine our actions, our reactions and the reasons for what we did. We ask our self, "Why did I do that?" We are likely doing better than we realize. This is important to acknowledge.

We must work through the 10th Gate regularly, even if we are feeling good. Otherwise, we will pass back through the Gate of Complacency, which takes us in the opposite direction of the 10th Gate of Awareness. It takes us back to Nowhere.

All of the Gates have their opposites and we can make a U-turn if we do not use self-discipline. However, we can always call on our True Power for help, just like the scarecrow and the tin woodsman did in the field of poppies. When Glinda performed a miracle by causing it to snow, the group awakened and continued their journey. If we perform the gratitude inventory, it will make all the difference to our motivation. That is one important reason to include it in our daily habits.

It is also demonstrated that we will assuredly find the solutions to our problems if we have an optimistic attitude. The solution might exist right under our nose. But, if we do not believe that we will find a solution, we will certainly not find it. Again we prove our self to be right. Do we want to be right or do we want to be happy? Actually, if we choose correctly we can be both. This means a 'win-win' for all involved.

One day, while I was writing this book, my neck began to stiffen up. I had been staring at the computer screen for hours. I wondered how I would finish this book without straining my eyes. Then I affirmed that my True Power would make it easy because I am carrying out my

True Power's will. Suddenly, I realized that I own a pair of glasses that are specifically for computer use. But I had forgotten about them. They were sitting right on my desk. In affirming the positive, I found that the solution was literally right under my nose. I could almost hear my True Power and guides laughing, "Right under your nose." They can have quite a sense of humor. Just laugh with them.

More and more data is being published to demonstrate how the mind creates our reality. This doesn't mean that, if we make mistakes in our thinking (which we will), our world will suddenly turn chaotic. Like most people, we have, at times, allowed our mind to run rampant, like an untrained dog. But we have survived. We do not judge our self and don't take our self too seriously. If we work through the 10th Gate regularly, we will always be able to find our way out of the Nightmare of Nowhere. The 11th Gate will then secure for us a more solid foundation in the happy dream.

We can always call on our True Power for help, just like the scarecrow and the tin woodsman did in the field of poppies. This is the first part of the 11th Gate. It will secure for us a more solid foundation in the happy dream, giving us previously unattainable power. When we have formally finished the 10th Gate we can confidently approach the 11th Gate – the Gate of Power.

~~~~~~~~~~~~~~~~~~~~~~~~~~~~~~~~~~~~

We can't know about that which we don't know exists.

- MA LAXMI ANAND

~~~~~~~~~~~~~~~~~~~~~~~~~~~~~~~~~~~~

Gate 11: Power

We sought through prayer and meditation to improve our conscious contact with our True Power, praying only for knowledge of its will for us and the power to carry that out.

The 11th Gate is truly the Gate of Power. It is the second of the three Maintenance Gates. Its opposite is the Gate of Weakness. There is so much to be said about this Gate that I will not even begin here, except to say that it is the most important of the Rainbow Gates because it can lead us to all the other Gates. Indeed, we can even begin the program at this Gate. The 11th Step of the AA program is largely kept in its original state, except that the title, "True Power," has been substituted for "God."[37]

Dorothy's tribe reached the Gate of Emerald City. They knocked on the door, asking for entry. At first, the Gatekeeper denied them entry. Supposedly, it was because they knocked when they should have rung the bell. After the Gatekeeper saw Dorothy's slippers (this was her connection with Glinda), they were allowed to enter. They were then prepared to meet the wizard.

In preparation, Dorothy received a new dress, the rust was removed from the tin man, the scarecrow received new stuffing and the lion was pampered. Even

---

[37] © *Alcoholics Anonymous*, Fourth Edition, page 59, reprinted with permission of Alcoholics Anonymous World Services, Inc.

Toto received a bow for his hair. They were prepared to have contact, to receive knowledge and, hopefully, to receive the gifts they truly desired. Unfortunately, the wizard demanded the wicked witch's broom before they could receive their gifts.

Knocking at the door of the Emerald City is symbolic of trying to engage with our True Power. We may not get it right on the first try, but we re-evaluate and try again. Some days we may not get past the Gatekeeper. That's okay.

Also, notice that the Gatekeeper let our friends in when he saw Dorothy's connection with Glinda. This is exemplified by Dorothy's slippers in the story but, for us, it will usually be the passage through the previous Gates, which prepare us for this all important event. The wizard exemplifies the confusion or irritation that is sometimes experienced when communicating with our True Power, or even with our mentors and gurus. We come for gifts and they send us on a dodgy mission. In truth, no mission is valueless. However, it may be painful, especially if it exposes dark reflections that must be released before we can receive our gifts.

Many people see prayer only as a means to ask for things. But prayer is also an act of communion with our True Power. For instance, consider gratitude. A great place we can freely express our gratitude is in prayer. Gratitude is the catalyst for answered prayers. When we are grateful for what we have, impetus is given to the "asking process."

However, it's a little different in the 11th Gate. Notice it says we pray *only* for our knowledge of True Power's will for us and the power to carry that out. This steers us away from using prayer as a means to "get something," which can often reinforce the ego's need for *more*. Remember that our True Power exists outside of time and space. It holds a vision of our past, present and future, as well as of all of the probabilities. So we want to ask our True Power to share its ideal vision with us and to reveal to us how we should participate in it.

Our True Power already knows what we desire. This doesn't mean that we cannot ask for things. But we should always be very thoughtful about what we ask for or we might just have to ask for it to be removed later. We are very powerful. However we may not know what is for our highest good. That is one reason it is "safer" just to ask for knowledge of our True Power's will because it contains everyone's highest possible good. But we can feel free to thank our true power for blessing received - especially if we want more of them. Our True Power wants us to be happy. Our blocks to the awareness of love are actually the only hindrance to our perpetual happiness.

Believe that it is our innate right to feel good and to be joyful. How do we feel right now? Do we feel light and hopeful, or do we feel pressured and irritated? Positive feelings are a key ingredient in manifesting the desires of our heart. Gather up as much positivity as we can muster. Practice awareness of our feelings. Choose not to identify with unhelpful one. This will release much negativity. We might also ask that our feelings be transformed (Gate 7). At this point, our feelings can be constantly improved upon until we maintain a permanent state of joy.

Our True Power wants us to be happy. But it must also operate under a set of Universal Laws. There is extensive material on this concept, which is beyond the scope of this book. However, if we have been applying the Universal Laws of Attraction incorrectly, we may have thought that our True Power didn't care about our happiness or that it was completely powerless to help.

We also need to give our True Power our permission to act in our life by asking for help. Miracles happen when we give the divine the permission to act on our behalf or on someone else's behalf. Of course there are other factors like "positive action." Prayer "with feet" is very powerful. This refers to the 6th Gate of Willingness and doing what we can reasonably do in the situation. Then our True Power does for us what we cannot do for our self. Ironically, quite often, miracles are just the correct use of the Laws of Attraction.

Our mind's proper use of the Laws of Attraction is more powerful than the natural laws. This is the reason miracles can happen. So, when we pray, it is vital that we do so in the affirmative. For instance, ask our True Power for what we want, not for what we *don't* want. Otherwise, we will bring energy to what we don't want.

What we focus on grows. So pray, "I like…" or "I prefer…" instead of "I need…" or "I want…" Needing and wanting infers some kind of lack. It's subtle but, in the higher realms, it's significant. Unsatisfied desires are an experience that is better left un-affirmed. We ask for what we prefer, and then be flexible by saying, "this or something better manifests for the highest good of all." Our True Power already knows what we prefer and like. Lack *is* the illusion.

On the other hand, *we* don't always know what is best for us and our True Power won't give us something that might make us fearful. We may want that $120K a year job but, if the responsibilities make us break out in a sweat at the mere thought, then it may be a no-go for now. Work on the fear.

Of course, we do not consciously want to limit our True Power in manifesting something for us. Preferably, focus on inner content over specific form. Inner content can be how a trait makes us feel, or its inner character. For instance, instead of focusing on the desired physical appearance of a partner, bring into our consciousness the inner *characteristics* desired.

When we ask our True Power for what we prefer, we should be mindful about asking for specifics of form. If we ask for something specific in form, like "brown hair," we limit the options that our True Power has for us. This is okay if nothing else will do. But are we going to pass up the ideal twin flame for this life simply because of the color of their hair?

It is less limiting for our True Power when we are specific about the content of what we prefer. Content represents the intangible qualities of something. On the other hand, form is the tangible qualities. We might say in prayer, or in a vision board, "loving and compassionate." This is much less limiting to manifest. The person that has these qualities can have any hair color.

Now, asking for a specific person to fall in love with us is actually a form of witchcraft. No judgment. It does work but, sometimes, it works too well. The problem is the potential violation of the free will of another and the karma for that. There is also the possibility that, when we ask for something specific (in form), later we will likely wish to have it removed.

Also here's another vital tip: Even with intangible preferences, be mindful of what we're asking. For example, if we pray for patience, we will likely experience many situations in which we have to practice patience. Who needs patience when we are in the flow of our True Power? We will be patient automatically if we are in the flow of bliss, joy and love. That is what we would really like, right? So, ask for bliss, joy and love, instead of patience.

If we are feeling irritable and we just have to complain, we observe the negative thoughts as they are passing from us and let them go. We practice awareness because, like our Creator, we *are* consciousness. Simply choose not to attach to the thoughts and let them die a natural death. Ideally, do this with someone in a sacred space who will not support our attachments. We are less likely to manifest the negativity behind our complaint when we are being mindful and sincere by trying to move past a block. Recognize also that our complaint is a feeling, not a fact (unless we want it to manifest into a fact.) Better yet, communicate in the past tense. The past does not exist. So, for instance, we might say, "True Power, I have been feeling sad..."

It is fruitful to use the present tense (not future tense) to refer to things that we want to affirm, (e.g., joy, love, harmony and abundance). Even better, we do this while we thank our True Power with a strong feeling of gratitude - the stronger the better. For example, we might say, "Thank you for the great food, the productive day, my wonderful partner and the beautiful sky." Say,

"Thank you for my perfect job opportunity," instead of "I am looking forward to the job I will have." Bring the situation into the present.

We should be flexible and open to the means by which our True Power might fulfill our needs. Most people focus on form, thinking of paper money as the only form in which abundance and prosperity will show up. Nothing could be farther from the truth. Even if there is little money in my account, I eat like a millionaire. I have access to high quality food. That's abundance for me.

It is our inner feelings that give meaning to these forms. For example, we may want a convertible for that feeling of exhilaration and freedom. We associate that feeling with the convertible. So, when we are thinking about what we desire, focus on how we will feel and the intangible qualities (the content of the situation), more than on the form. Better yet, we focus on how it will make us *feel*.

That is not to say that a person or thing that we were specifically wishing for won't show up in our life. Certainly they can. That actually happened to me. But the point is to provide our True Power and the Universal Laws of Attraction with some leeway so that it can help us. We must trust that it will choose the perfect manifestation, surprising and delighting us.

If our True Power could give us something better than what we asked for, would we turn it down?

Nonetheless, many people limit their True Power to the extent that the answer will *seem* to be "no," when it is actually "not that particular one", "not just yet," or "Wow, Lydia you made manifesting this almost impossible. Can I have some leeway?" Sometimes, it seems more like crickets chirping (silence) rather than our True Power answering. That's what most people experience when they are missing some key information about their True Power. Like Oral Robert's motto states, "the feeling that 'something good is going to happen to us' ought to prevail."

There is no need to take back control from our True Power. It has the highest vision for our life. We have now developed a relationship with our True Power. We have worked through the Rainbow Gates, clearing our channel, so that we can easily utilize its vision for our life.

By working through this 11th Gate regularly, we will either gain more power or we will discover the power that we have always held. When we started this program, we *felt* powerless and our life *seemed* unmanageable. This is because we didn't know how to work with our True Power. So, often, we have been working *against* our True Power - and our self.

Prayer and meditation are skills that need development. So, once they are learned, they are disciplines that must be maintained. A potential pitfall is letting the ego take control of our will to the point that we lose the will (indecision) to cooperate with our True Power. This *will* be more painful than before the Gates. But, we don't beat our self up. That only strengthens the ego in a negative way. Experiencing contrast is part of the learning process.

It is through this contrasting experience that we will realize that we have been working against our self. Soon, we will begin to realize that we and our True Power have the same ideas, that we have the same tastes and that our will is the same. Eventually, we will realize that we *are* the same. We are one and the same. Words are insufficient to explain this.

When we ask for the help of our True Power, we will feel the power come in. We will become increasingly more sensitive to it. There will be a peace that we have never experienced before - a peace that cannot be shaken with the appearance of chaos. This is the joy that is continual and not fleeting.

We have developed a relationship with our True Power. We are now in the process of aligning our will with that of our True Power. It is appropriate to say that our will is changing and the will of our True Power will develop into our heart's desire. We have worked through the Rainbow Gates so that we can collaborate and utilize its vision for us.

Collaboration and communication with our True Power will be a joy for both of us. It longs to have our attention. Remember, we were created so that our True Power could love us and be with us. There may be times when our old desires for chaos or bad habits return. However, if we stay in close contact with our True Power, there will be an enormous amount of growth and learning, and even miracles.

In following our desires, it does not mean that those things won't bring lessons for growth. Surely, they will. But mostly they will bring love. Since marrying my twin flame, the love of my life, there are lots of lessons. These are ongoing because I'm not perfect, nor is he. He's the only person for whom I would endure these difficult lessons. But there is more love than lessons, making it so worthwhile. That's the reason my True Power needed me to be with him. I lovingly call him my "earthly entertainer." I'm his biggest fan and he is mine.

Our will is not taken away in this process and we do not become a saint. At least most of us do not. Indeed, we will start to find that desire is the carrot that is used by our True Power to guide us. We will find that, when we follow our heart, doors will open and our life will begin to flow. However, sometimes chaos ensues initially, as falsehoods fall away from our life. Our True Power does not want us to be a slave of any kind. That's why we are living this dream with *free* will.

Some of we have feared the manifesting of our desires, thinking there is always a price to pay. We couldn't trust our self; much less trust our own desires. But it is a new day. We have dealt with most of these problems by working through the previous Gates. The desires of our heart are now aligning with those of our True Power. We can now start to trust our self. This is the greatest gift - the return to our Self.

Earlier we talked about our True Power being so quiet that we have to listen for its still, small voice. That is the reason we need to sit quietly. It also shows our willingness to listen to our True Power after we have prayed to receive its guidance. It makes no sense to ask for guidance from our True Power, only to run around for the rest of the day making no attempt to listen to that voice. Think about this scenario...

A husband says to his wife, "Oh, I want to hear about our day." He then says to her, "Can we get to the point?" while he turns the volume up on the TV. He then forgets that he was talking to her because he is now absorbed in his television show. Essentially, his behavior is betraying his intentions, despite what he said.

Our relationship with our True Power is a relationship just like any other. It needs to be nurtured. If we must jump up and go, we can be mindful while we're on the go. Just acknowledge our True Power and be aware of our surroundings and our experience (inward awareness).

However, we must dedicate some time to meditational practice in order to maintain and make progress. Just quiet our mind so that we can be a channel for the guidance and power of our True Power. Practice awareness for that is what We are. Many people make this a ritual in the morning, to start their day. It is beneficial to make conscious contact with our True Power on a daily basis – ideally, with no reservations.

Our True Power will mostly commune with us through right brain activity. This includes language, feelings, images, dreams, movement, music and art, etc. It will be a different experience for everyone. We will come to understand how our True Power talks to us personally.

There are probably many groups in our city that we can attend to learn about meditation. If not, there are many books, seminars, webinars and courses on the topic. There are many resources that we can tap into to learn to quiet our mind so that we can establish a conscious contact with our True Power.

Many people find that a seated form of meditation does not work for them. Some people discover communion with their True Power when they run or jog. Some find their True Power through music or writing, or some other creative outlet. It is very personal, but we will likely find something that comes naturally to us.

After we have regularly visited the 11th Gate of Power for a while, we will begin to trust our self more. This is as it should be. We might need to talk about this with others, just to make sure that we are staying on track and not being reckless - or delusional. This sometimes happens when we are still learning how to follow our True Power. It's nothing to be alarmed or embarrassed about. Just get back on track.

Our desires are generally safe, as long as they are not threatening to our physical or mental health, and as long as they are not perceived by others to be harmful. Some say, "if it's practical, it's spiritual." Others say, "when in doubt, don't." We need to define what feels safe and sane to us. My motto is "if I don't want to try something simply because I'm afraid, then I try to move forward with it asking for the fear to be removed." If I really just dislike an idea, but have no fear of it, then it's a no-go. As we grow and evolve spiritually, both thoughts and behaviors will be continually redefined. But there are many pitfalls at the beginning, so we should have a mentor, preacher, teacher, friend or guru to offer us advice when it is needed.

The Rainbow Gates program is a process of spiritual advancement. It takes us back to our self - to our True Power. This is accomplished by developing a deep and trusting relationship with our True Power. It is our ultimate authority. But trusting in it can feel very risky at times. There might be times when others think that we are foolish for acting upon what our True Power reveals to us. In time, when our relationship with our True Power is firmly established, we will be able to take "risks" without consulting others, unless of course they are directly affected, such as our partner.

No one can truly tell us how this Gate will work for us because our relationship with our True Power is so unique and sacred that, to comment excessively on it may limit its potential. However, for maximum effectiveness, this Gate should be worked through daily.

Many people have experienced instant, brilliant, spiritual awakenings, while working through this Gate. We might receive in milliseconds the answers to problems that were previously not solvable by us. For others, it might take years to gather substantial insight. But we will always benefit from the emotional balance in the 11th Gate and that is invaluable. We will achieve as much spiritual ground as we desire and as much as we believe we can have. Remember that we have a Super-Power in our back pocket.

The previous Gates have paved the way for us to be a clear and powerful channel for our True Power. After passing through them we succeed with more advanced spiritual endeavors. Prayer and meditation will become very comforting. It is these two disciplines that will accelerate our growth in other spiritual endeavors.

Indeed, it is the basis for almost any advanced spiritual practice. Our beliefs and our personal preferences will determine how we express our spirituality in this Gate.

Our will is now aligned with the will of our True Power. We may "hear" it actually speak to us (with inner hearing). Usually, it does this by guiding us through the desires of our heart. I receive guidance via images (usually inner), intuition, premonitions, feelings, esoteric and detailed wisdom, desires of the heart and inner auditory messages. Clarity is gained by exercising the 10th and 11th Gates. We trust our self. Our desires no longer betray us. This is a gift in itself, but we have found a new use for our desires. They are messages from our True Power.

Another gift is that we now see our self differently. We are more compassionate. Our relationships have likely improved. We look forward to the future, knowing that the desires of our heart carry a long-term plan for we, co-created by we and our True Power. Our True Power will guide us step by step, every day, because it knows the master plan. It will usually only give us the information that is necessary. Usually, we will have to take action on that information before more is given. For instance, when I am given a list of topics to record videos about, generally, I am not given more topics until I have completed the recording of those videos.

We might pray when we are hurting, but if we also pray habitually upon awakening and throughout the day, we will attain the level of peace, love and joy that we desire. This basically means that we should acknowledge our True Power throughout the day. The best way to do that is with gratitude. For instance, say "Thank you True Power for this food," "Thank-you for this pretty flower." It is *we* who are in control of how much peace, love and joy we want to experience. President Abraham Lincoln said that people are about as happy as they want to be.

One of the main benefits for working through this Gate is the balancing of our emotional state. There is a certain range of emotions that we can live out comfortably while we are alive.

Basically, there are differences between sympathy and compassion, anxiety and anticipation, happiness and joy, lust and love, excitement and exhilaration. The latter of these emotions, like compassion and joy, are of a higher frequency and have no repercussions that require negative balancing. However, the former emotions, like excitement and anxiety, require balance from their opposite because they are lower frequency. A good way to describe the emotional boomerang is "what goes up must come down." We learn to discern when our emotions signal that we have returned to the Nightmare.

The results of prayer and meditation will certainly show up in our life. We are free to be whom and what we want to be. We are free to do what we want to do - when we want to do it. This doesn't mean that we don't have to pick up a shovel, nor will we necessarily become an instant millionaire. But we *can* be, if we want to be. What is most important is that we will *feel* like a millionaire. "I feel like a million bucks." That is the point of being a millionaire, isn't it?

Isn't the real reason for having money, cars and beautiful things so that we can enjoy the feelings they engender, like freedom and joy? Well, we can have the *feelings* of freedom and joy right now. Try it. We practice feeling good. It is "The Secret". Ironically, we will attain abundance and prosperity much more rapidly as we *contain* positive feelings.

This is the opposite of the idea that "desperate people do desperate things." When we begin to trust that our life is going well, we are more open to people. Likewise, "loving people do loving things." Life loves us back. More precisely, it is *us* who love us back. When the blocks to the awareness of the love that surrounds us have been removed, we live in a more loving way. We will feel that love. Life expresses the love that we are and have always been. We become naturally loving.

A rose does nothing per se. It just is. It is just the symbol of passionate love. Certainly, countless people have felt loved in the presence of a rose. We are that rose. Love is our meaning. We can extend our love and joy merely by "being." Those who are receptive to it will feel it positively. Others may be irritated by our "rosiness." That's okay.

We will begin to allow other people to be whom and what they are, without needing them to change so that we are comfortable. We can't directly control others. Anyway, we are not losing control. Control is only an illusion that we had any. The good news is that we and others can be the recipient of a miracle. Ask our True Power to show us a different perspective. We will either be given the ability to accept things the way they are or we will watch as the "problem" disappears entirely. Acceptance precedes the miracle.

We have now arrived at the bridging point of this book. We have reached the point in our spiritual growth at which the Universal Laws of Attraction will start to work almost magically for us. Certainly we will be guided to take action and we will enjoy the action that we take. Our affirmations will become very powerful. We will start to see manifestations much more quickly. We may have already experienced this.

Being the seeker that we are, we were probably experimenting with many religions and philosophies prior to working through these Rainbow Gates. We might have ended up more perplexed and hopeless after our experience with them. But we are wholeheartedly encouraged to pursue those interests again.

Everything seems different in the Nightmare of Nowhere – darker, chaotic and senseless. But now we have a different 'state of mind.' Now we perceive from a new place. Things that did not work before will work now. Affirmations that previously fell flat will produce effects – sometimes extremely quickly. Our desires will manifest before we even tell anyone about them.

Our True Power knows the desires of our heart and has always been eager to please us. All we needed to know was where our power was, how it operates and under what laws it does so.

In this 11th Gate we often receive daily marching orders and clear messages about the day's tasks. We will find that our day flows and we are productive. There are many coincidences and miracles happening in our life now. Even when challenges appear, we fly like a bird, far above troubled waters.

The conscious contact that we can achieve with our True Power is now significantly more powerful and effective than it was before we worked through these 12 Rainbow Gates. At this point, our conscious contact will grow and deepen. We can truly feel good about what we have accomplished.

This is the Rainbow Bridge that we have been building. Now we can cross it. We are securing our place in the land of light. There is no limit to what we can achieve, as long as we regularly work through the Maintenance Gates.

It is time to share this spiritual awakening and love with others. This will ensure that we keep and expand on our freedom. That is the purpose of the final Gate.

~~~~~~~~~~~~~~~~~~~~~~~~~~~~~~

"Love cannot be explained for it is beyond explanation." - ACIM

~~~~~~~~~~~~~~~~~~~~~~~~~~~~~~

Gate 12: Service

Having had a spiritual awakening we continued to practice these principles in all our affairs.

The 12th and final Gate is called the Gate of Service. This is the last of the Gates. Its opposite is the Gate of Self. The entire section of the original 12-step that begins with the phrase "we tried to carry this message to..." was removed from the 12th Gate because the phrase "practicing these principles in all or affairs" seems to include this concept of love and service.

Service is a great way to instill what we have learned and need to learn. It is a way to prove to our self that we do indeed have certain gifts. Just like the scarecrow, tin man and lion who exemplified their gifts. They were unaware of their gifts until the wizard showed them that they had them all along.

How do we know we're intelligent until we solve a conundrum? How do we know we're compassionate until we feel our heart strings pulled? How do we know if we're a leader until we've led? We don't. But, if we can give calmness, security, inspiration or happiness to someone, then we must have it to give. We cannot give away what we do not have to give. Put another way, we are simply unaware of what we have until we give it.

Service can be as simple as giving someone our smile. Are others made happier by our presence? Never mind that we might be irritated by theirs. If they are happier, then that is a gift that we have the ability to give. Now we give it to our self.

We may want to be helpful but may not know how to be helpful. Just as we cannot judge what is best for our self, we leave it to our True Power to do so. It can see the future, the past and all probable realities. Our True Power will guide us specifically with each situation that we ask for guidance. Two situations can appear completely the same but we may be guided to act completely differently in each situation. Help others with no expectation of return. Share and help for the sheer joy of it. There is a reason this Gate is not passed through earlier.

It is important to acknowledge when our True Power guides us to be involved in service and when it does not. People who are just starting their recovery are admonished to do small things, such as stacking chairs and making coffee. It is a lack of humility to do service beyond our ability to be helpful. That is the reason that, when we are acting as another person's spiritual advisor, it is helpful to consult our own spiritual advisor. Otherwise, we could unwittingly be unhelpful, and then likely have to make amends.

Keep in mind that there have been major revisions to the 12 Steps of the AA[38] program in order to transform

---

[38] © *Alcoholics Anonymous*, Fourth Edition, page 59, reprinted with permission of

them into the 12 Rainbow Gates. As they were revised, it seemed that my own True Power called for more revisions. As I have learned, it is best to listen.

As Dorothy's troupe took Emerald City they became the talk of the town. But they were not so important that the wizard of Oz gave them their gifts and the keys to Emerald City upon arrival. He asked the troupe of five to bring him the broom that belongs to the wicked witch. In returning to the dark forest, Dorothy and Toto are captured. After Toto escapes and shows them where they can find Dorothy, her friends come to her rescue. She throws water on the witch in order to save the scarecrow. The wicked witch melts, her minions are set free and Dorothy brings the broom back to the wizard. Only then does the wizard reveal the gifts that are desired by Dorothy's group.

We are now well prepared to help others leave Nowhere. But remember that, in order to do that, we might be led *back* to the Nightmare of Nowhere, just as Dorothy and the others were. There is a story about a very wise man who, after his ascension, descended into the lower depths to retrieve others. He said, "And greater things than these shall you do." Indeed, we will do greater things. We will need to do so in order to keep what we have gained.

Alcoholics Anonymous World Services, Inc.

We may not know the reason we feel guided to do something, or why we get a sudden craving, but synchronicity happens. We will be helpful beyond measure if we stay open. Indeed, we will never see the vast healing ripples in the pond that we create when we follow our True Power's guidance. Follow our heart.

When we advance in our spiritual practice we will actually find that we will be led to places to help others. This is when our True Power needs our help. It is now about helping to meet the needs of others too. We have true collaboration and cooperation with our True Power. Our True Power has been taking care of us. We live in a flow that is not yet common in this world. Now we can share the joy that it brings.

The Gate of Service is for *our* joy. It may even be our passion. When we began the Rainbow Gates, we probably just wanted to find a better way to live. We might not have been seeking a spiritual awakening. Nonetheless, that is what was required to bring us to this point. Our partnership with our True Power sustains us. Now is our chance to give back.

Before we did the work of looking inward, we may have tried to help others and found it didn't turn out well usually. So what is different now? There is a difference between helping someone and hobbling them. There is a difference between giving out of abundance and joy, and giving out of lack. Basically, give of our overflow from the "cup of life." But we do not leave our self feeling deprived.

Always give without any expectation of return or results. Giving with the expectation of some particular result is another pitfall. Just do the footwork and leave the results to our True Power. This idea can be applied to so much of our lives. Just let go and let God. The reward is in the action itself. Expect nothing from it in return. Otherwise, it's just a contract - not service work. In other words, we don't help someone if we think that we might become resentful if they don't reciprocate in some way or complete the goal that we had for them.

We have a physical body, so our True Power needs us to perform those tasks that require hands, feet, sight, talent, communication, movement and so on. It will need us to be its tool or vessel. There are certain things that our True Power will lead us to do.

At this point we might feel reluctant to continue. We might think that we don't have time to do things for others. Well, we will not be required to give up our life and leave the country to go on a missionary expedition. Our True Power is not going to ask us to do anything that we do not want to do. But, keep an open mind about service to others.

I am living my passion right now, as I write this book. I don't know whom it might help, but I am thoroughly enjoying myself as I write it. The reward is in the action itself. So I have my reward already. When we follow the guidance of our True Power, we let go of the outcome. We expect nothing in return. When we give in this manner, we have an extraordinary amount of power to help others.

The 12th Gate is about opening to "the flow" and recognizing our self in others. Be receptive to whether or not people are open to the ideas that we're presenting. Share only our experience, strength and hope, and we will find that others will be much more receptive. Sharing this way is not proselytizing.   It is attraction, not promotion. Keep in mind that everyone has their own True Power.

Helping and sharing is an opportunity for us to keep what we have. Just be open and willing to do so. Don't base our efforts on results. Just do the footwork and let go of the results. There are many ways for others to find their own Path. Somebody might want us to accompany them to a spiritual gathering or to a Rainbow Gate meeting. But it is always us who grows.

When we help others in service work, don't focus on people who don't want to hear the message. Focus on those who want what we have to give. Love those who truly want to be loved. Don't push love on those who don't want it, *even* if they are our family members. Spread love beyond our family and friends - because we are *all* family.

I've heard people comment on the sense of humor that their True Power has. Unfortunately, that humor usually rests in the irony of karmic lessons. If I judge someone, it won't be long before I'm on the other side of the fence re-learning the fact that I am *incapable* of judgment.

On another note, be careful when offering advice to people. I, myself, have been known to say, "If I wanted our opinion, I would've paid you for it." Frankly, it's the way I felt at the time. I'm sharing this with you because there is a need to be sensitive to the ego in people. I was irritated by people who overtly gave me advice. Nonetheless, since you are reading this book, it is assumed that you are interested in *my* advice.

At any point in a conversation, the other party might have heard enough (at least the ego will have heard enough). They will have absorbed as much as they can at that time. So know when to stop talking and do so with a smile. We will want to keep the relationship friendly so that they will talk with us again if they want to know more. Again, the safest way to offer information is to share our experience, strength and hope. If we want to share our opinions widely, we can publish a book.

We have now developed a conscious connection with our True Power, which opens us to receive truthful information - lots of it. We are like a computer with high speed Internet now. We have access to more and more information. That is one of the benefits of spiritual growth. However, we will find that not everyone will be so eager to hear this information. They might become bored or irritated, especially those who are close to us. It's not personal.

Supposedly, even Jesus was an irritant to people in his own hometown. Can you imagine a neighborhood kid turning birds into stone and drying up fruit trees? You can almost hear the neighbors, "Keep your Jesus kid out of my garden. He already cursed one of my fig trees."

Similarly, the Buddha left home in the middle of the night; right after his son was born. Think of how his queen felt? She probably said to her maids, "Buddhism-my butt. Siddhartha is just a spoiled little prince who wants to roam the countryside." Hey, it's a valid point. It may be very difficult for others to understand people who follow their inner guidance. So we must try to be patient with those who are close to us and, at the same time, not abandon our inner knowing and guidance.

Try to find an outlet for the download of information we receive during meditation. The 10th Gate is a great place to record this information. Find other spiritual groups or form a Rainbow Gates group. Spiritual awakenings look very different for everyone. But certain traits are common among all of them.

The promises of the AA program[39], which are listed in a previous chapter, actually embody our new experience. Although they are bold and astounding promises, many members of the AA program attest to their validity. There is a sense of connection to life and to others, and an end to loneliness and isolation. This is what is known as "self-actualization."

Maslow's Hierarchy is a theory in psychology that was proposed by Abraham Maslow in 1943. It lists the following "needs" as a way to describe a pattern of motivation that human beings move through, one by one. The current level must be fulfilled before someone will focus on the next level. The final level is self-actualization. This is how the void is filled.

- Physiological
- Safety
- Belonging and Love
- Esteem
- Self-Actualization

When we regularly pass through the 12th Gate, we experience a growing sense of peace. There is less negative thought about our self and our image. We focus more lovingly on others. Indeed, sensitivity to the feelings of others will ensure that we maintain the progress we have made.

---

[39] © *Alcoholics Anonymous,* Fourth Edition, page 83-84, reprinted with permission of Alcoholics Anonymous World Services, Inc.

Part of the original 12th Step of AA was omitted. It states, "We carried this message to others"[40] people. Nobody likes to be preached to, especially these days. It can be the quickest way to push somebody away. On the other hand, we should stay open to people who want we to give them information about what we believe.

One of the best ways we can share our beliefs is by being an example. How do we present our self to others? Do we have a puckered brow? Are we skulking about? (Yes, *skulking* is a real word.) People will notice when we walk into a room, shining our light. They will want to know what we're doing because they want something we have. That's good. If we're eating in a restaurant, with friends who are laughing like the people that are described in the beginning of this book, some people will think, "Hey, I'll have whatever they are having." Still others will just wish we'd be quiet. That's okay – we're happy.

Don't make the mistake of thinking that we can fake happiness. People know. As a matter of fact, people also know when we gossip about them. When we gossip about others, they feel it. More importantly, gossip will affect our spiritual progress. If we have to talk about someone, do it with great respect and with sincerity. These kinds of changes are required for those who want

---

40 © *Alcoholics Anonymous*, Fourth Edition, page 60, reprinted with permission of Alcoholics Anonymous World Services, Inc.

to advance spiritually. Sensitivity to the feelings of others will ensure that we maintain the progress we have made.

Keep moving forward in pursuit of higher spiritual ground. If we find that we are becoming bored, ask for more direction and guidance from our True Power. Living joyfully is never boring. Boredom is a sign that we are sliding back into the Nightmare of Nowhere. It's our nemesis. We progress spiritually when we practice the principles of the Rainbow Gates, (i.e., honesty, open-mindedness, trust, cooperation, self-knowledge, humbleness, willingness, purification, thoughtfulness, love, awareness, power, and service).

In the same way that negativity has touched every area of our life, spiritual enlightenment touches every area of our life too. We know that life is worth living and we are glad to be alive. We feel love for our self and for others. We find new creative outlets and passions. We do things that we didn't have the energy, time or means to do previously. We gain self-respect.

Self-respect, or pride, is thought to be the opposite of humility. But the word *humility* is often misunderstood. It does not mean that we belittle or invalidate our self, but that we see our self in right relationship to our True Power. We know what our True Power can and cannot do. We know what *we* can and cannot do. There is no role confusion. Both of we have our own roles. Humility is the correct perspective of our self in relation to our True Power.

Miracles will stop happening if we confuse our role with the role of our True Power. But remember that pain is the warning sign that calls for us to pay attention so that we can remedy the situation - and now we know how.

Aiding others on their spiritual journey will bring another level of empowerment. As we help others, our True Power will increasingly be able to help us. In time, we might find creative ways in which we can aid others on their spiritual journey. Maybe we would like to write a book, or paint or write poetry. Maybe we would like to teach a class or volunteer at a food bank. Maybe our calling is to be a statistician or engineer. Maybe we need to engineer the Underground Railroad out of Nowhere.

The best thing about our spiritual awakening is the relationship we will have with our True Power. There is nothing that fills the emptiness like that relationship. Indeed, the emptiness is the shape of our True Power. Although our True Power will send us abundant signs of its love in our outer world, our inner world will be the most fulfilling.

Having a fulfilling relationship with our True Power will also deepen our relationship with our twin flame – our soul mate. If we are not already with that person, it will prepare us to meet that person if that is what we truly desire.

We might meet that person because we need their support as we work on our deepest life lessons. Dare I say that they can provide us with some of our greatest lessons. This happened to me in a magical way. I saw my twin flame and my life changed forever. Certainly, there were major existential lessons surrounding the meeting of my twin flame and in being with him. But the love always prevails. It is the centerpiece of our relationship, even after 15 years. We just like being with each other. ACIM calls this person "the One." But thine eye must be single. The Rainbow Gates will help refine our desires so they are in balance, not in conflict.

Progressively, we are spiritually renewed and enlightened. Insights will deepen and wisdom will grow into understanding and knowing. Questions will be answered as they arise. We realize that problems come with solutions.

Now that we have found our way to freedom, we can go wherever we like. As long as we make decisions with the help of our True Power, we will have a good day. Even hard days are good because we have ceased fighting anything and anyone. We are grateful to have escaped. Gravity will not have the same effect on us. It is a new life in a new place. What is this new place in which we now live? In the Land of Oz it is called the Emerald City. Here, it's the happy dream.

~~~~~~~~~~~~~~~~~~~~~~~~~~~~~~

"Knowing others is intelligence; knowing yourself is true wisdom. Mastering others is strength; mastering yourself is true power."

– Lao-Tzu

~~~~~~~~~~~~~~~~~~~~~~~~~~~~~~

The Gates Back to Nowhere

We are now spending less and less time in the Nightmare of Nowhere and the light is getting infinitely brighter. We are free to return to the Nightmare of Nowhere at will. But we don't ever have to be a permanent resident again. We have been freed and we now know how to get out. Time is not kind in the nightmare. So live as much as we can in the happy dream.

The longer we live in the light; it becomes increasingly more painful to experience the darkness. We will know when we are Nowhere because things will suddenly become chaotic, darker and less loving. Acknowledge it and earnestly prepare to re-escape the tyrannical rule. Any success requires great effort. If we stay a long time, it might be hard to escape. That was my experience.

The first time I escaped from Nowhere, I was given a lot of grace and it was a breeze. But I didn't realize what was given to me. I didn't realize that it was a gift. When I returned to Nowhere, I was in the dark forest for five years. It is so painful to be so sad when we have known such happiness. I had to really work to get out. I practically clawed my way back out because I knew I had to or I would die. We can tell if we have returned to Nowhere by asking our self the following questions:

- How do I feel overall? Why do I feel this way?
- What thoughts or events triggered this feeling?
- What memories does this feeling bring up?
- Have I acted unloving?
- Do I need to make amends?

Remember to take along our tools. If we suddenly find our self back in Nowhere, here's a quick remedy list from the Gates of things we should remember to do:

- Admit (at least to our self) that we are feeling something we don't like. (Gate 1)
- Trust our True Power and decide to cooperate with it. (Gates 2 and 3)
- Let go of our decision to see things a certain way. Take a mini-inventory. If we need to talk with someone, do so. (Gates 4 and 5)
- Decide that we would rather be happy than be right. What is there to lose? (Gate 6)
- Ask our True Power to take us out of Nowhere and help us to wake up. This is the same as being awakened from a "bad" dream. Indeed, that is what is happening. (Gate 7)
- If we need to make amends, do so quickly. (Gate 8 and 9)

Beware the Gates that lead us Nowhere. They are mirror opposites of the Gates that led us *out*:

- Gate 12: The Gate of Self
- Gate 11: The Gate of Weakness
- Gate 10: The Gate of Complacency
- Gate 9: The Gate of Fear
- Gate 8: The Gate of Thoughtlessness
- Gate 7: The Gate of Contamination
- Gate 6: The Gate of Reluctance
- Gate 5: The Gate of Pride
- Gate 4: The Gate of Denial
- Gate 3: The Gate of Resistance
- Gate 2: The Gate of Distrust
- Gate 1: The Gate of Delusion

Slipping backward, we would begin a return to Nowhere through Gate 12 first – the Gate of Self. We would completely give up doing any service or having a mind for helping others. We become completely absorbed in our self and our problems.

At times, it is appropriate to be absorbed in helping only our self. Self-care is important. But try to return to our passions, purpose and service, as soon as possible. Doing what we have a passion for relieves us of the bondage of self. Do we do things for others, without expecting anything in return? There is a place for healthy boundaries, but we need to make time to give back to others regularly in some way. We will remember what we have by first giving it away. That is also how we keep it. We realize that we are love because we can give love. We wouldn't be able to give love if we didn't *have* it to give.

The next Gate back to Nowhere is the 11th Gate - the Gate of Weakness. This Gate corresponds inversely to the Gate of True Power. Going back through this Gate will eventually be catastrophic to our peace of mind. Knowledge is power. True knowledge is True Power. So, if we are not receiving this knowledge on a regular basis, we are like a blind man walking in the dark forest.

The forest is an awesome place, but not for a blind person. It might be exciting for a little while but, when a snake crosses our Path (and they will because it's the forest), it will be problematic. Don't get angry at the snake. They live there. We just need to know which way to go to avoid the snake. If we're not communing with our True Power, we will miss that information. This is not to say that we don't have snakes or other problems when we are practicing the Gate of Power. But we have the power, assistance and knowledge to handle the challenge.

The Gate of Complacency mirrors the Gate of Awareness. If we pass back through this Gate of Complacency, we have stopped being the beholder and practicing gratitude. Also, when we stop making personal amends, it can begin to seem like others are pitted against us. But, in truth, we are just projecting our stubborn position onto them.

Again, remember that clinical research has shown that an attitude of gratitude improves depression, accuracy in thinking and productivity. Just thinking of three new things for which we are grateful every day can shift our world view - literally.

If we have passed the three Maintenance Gates, we will automatically enter the Gate of Fear. Fear is something that might not have been completely eliminated after working the 12th Gate. However, it will have been greatly diminished and manageable. Remember that, although love has no opposite Elsewhere, fear is the opposite of love in Nowhere.

There is a difference between *feeling* fear and *acting* upon it. In the Gate of Fear, we will begin to act on our fears. Not responding to fear is having courage. Acting on fear only brings more fear. If we do not turn around at this point, we will progress quickly to the Gate of Thoughtlessness. This is the mirror opposite of the Gate of Thoughtfulness, which is when we prepare to make amends. Depending on the level of involvement, amending relationships can be a continual process. It is the act of being thoughtful and loving.

Being loving is an attitude. If we behave lovingly, we are being thoughtful toward another. Conversely, having passed through the Gate of Fear, we will act in a self-serving manner and we will only be able to think of our self. Self-care is good, but not at the expense of others. Basically, this means that we will have an uncaring attitude and we will become thoughtless of others. In Anonymous groups, it is referred to as self-centered fear. This is the source of much anguish. This means that I become afraid that I won't get something I want or that I will lose something I have. Think about the things we've been afraid of losing or not getting.

In seeking our own self-interests, we could even seriously cause another person pain. Although harm is an illusion, pain is an experience. Therefore, to the other person, it is *very* real.

At this point, unless we turn around, we will enter the Gate of Contamination. This Gate is the mirror opposite of the 7th Gate of Purification. If we have been acting out of fear and we have hurt our self or others, an undesirable character trait will be revived. This might be related to our actions, beliefs or attitudes. For instance, one person might return to overeating or smoking; another might become suspicious of others or have extramarital affairs; yet another might become irritable and depressed. Contamination has started to recur. It might take a little time, but that will happen unless spiritual progress is resumed. This is because we are essentially "marked." We have been called and we have answered the call. There is no going back to the nightmare without experiencing intense pain. This is not an empty threat. It has been the experience of those traveling this Path.

Although this is a common phenomenon for people in recovery, it applies to everyone. Addiction and alcoholism are simply extreme examples of symptoms of being "marked". Interestingly, in order to recover from an addiction, recovering people often have to maintain a very high level of integrity.

If we have not turned around at this point, we will enter the Gate of Reluctance. Just like going through the 6th Gate of Willingness, this is going to entail pain that needs relief. Indeed we may go to great lengths to escape it. Then we will need to substantiate our position by going through the Gate of "False" Pride, which is the mirror of the 5th Gate of Humbleness. We will need to really bolster to our self about the reason why our actions and positions are "right." Thus we will begin to rationalize what we are doing. We will also tend to keep secrets, which is a symptom of pride. And as they declare in NA, "we are only as sick as our secrets."

This is not to say that we will need to tell everyone our personal business. People who have a low sense of integrity and who have no desire to live outside of Nowhere are not the people who are safe to confide in. We will just be drawn further into the Nightmare of Nowhere. Instead, we have someone we can turn to who has gone down this Path and who has maintained a high level of integrity. Essentially, we will feel alone if we do not have at least one person who knows our secrets. But I digress.

Now, if we have not returned from the Gate of Pride, our mind will lead us into the Gate of Denial. That is how our mind fixes incongruity within it. We will be in denial that we have done anything to delay our return to happiness. We will think that we are a victim of the system, the boss, our spouse, our family or whatever.

The Gate of Denial is the mirror of the 4th Gate of Self-Knowledge. This implies that we will begin to lose sight of the part we play in our own life. We will then go through the Gate of Resistance. We will deny the responsibilities in our life. We will not be cooperating with our True Power and the laws under which it operates. Not only will we be unconsciously working against our True Power, but we will resist it, more or less.

Then, something truly amazing will happen on the way back to the Nightmare of Nowhere. We will blame our True Power for being careless. Suddenly and subtly, we cannot understand this "power" anymore and we doubt it even *has* so-called power, let alone love. We have entered the Gate of Distrust. It is the mirror opposite of the 2nd Gate of Trust.

If we do not turn around now and we continue to substantiate our position, we will be living in the

Nightmare of Nowhere for a while. We have re-entered the nightmare through the Gate of Delusion - the mirror opposite of the 1st Gate of Illusion.

Unlike the Gate of Illusion, we will be rationalizing our perceptions as real. We will not give up our illusions. In fact, we are justifying them, complaining about others and railing at the world. We believe we have little to no responsibility in this outcome. No, it is everyone else's fault. Nothing makes sense. We do not understand how our world became so messed up. We will reason, "I hate it here, but it makes more sense than their BS."

We are sure that the people that talk about peace and love are "full of it" and that they are just "blowing hot air." They are just trying to make themselves feel better. We have convinced our self that there is no real science behind the universal laws, or our True Power, Higher Powers, God or otherwise.

The reason this is called the Gate of Delusion is that, when we are in this Gate, we actually *defend* our illusions. When we completely return to the Nightmare of Nowhere, essentially, we give up hope. We may have to endure quite a lot before we will even consider going back through the Rainbow Gates.

The last time this happened to me, it took me five years to change my mind. I went into a darkness that I had never experienced before. I was classified as disabled. When I approached the Gates again, I hated the idea of God. I went to a meeting railing, "Do you know what God let happen to my kids? I hate God. I'm a better god than that." I needed a new perspective. I needed my True Power. But my True Power had never left me. It was patiently waiting for my return.

We do not have to believe in a God outside of our self. Buddhists believe in their own innate ability to free themselves from internal turmoil and to find peace with their perceptions of the world. However, if we do believe in a God that exists outside of our self, that works equally well. It has its own set of benefits. We might be able to tap into a deep well of belief in a very great power, which might bring about situations that would not happen if we believed otherwise. Either way, we will be right.

Why is that? Because this is *our* world and what we say goes. That is, if we really believe it. Similarly, if we believe that this world is awful and that there is no rhyme or reason to it, we will be right again. We will be right until we decide that we want to see it another way. We're in charge here.

We are always in charge. The Universe loves us that much. In fact, *we* love us that much and, if we believe in our True Power, it loves us that much too. Nothing can intrude on our will in reality. Depending on our perception, we are either a Creator or we are a co-creator.

Do we believe that we existed before we incarnated here? If we don't, we might have a sense that we were thrown into this "thing" against our will. We have probably said, "I didn't ask for these parents. I didn't ask to be treated this way. Who would do that?" No judgment. I've been there, done that and said that.

Whatever we believe, we will find evidence for. But, if it leaves us feeling sick inside, it isn't mirroring reality. Thoughts that more closely mirror reality, the happy dream, will leave us feeling hopeful, healthier and happier. Thoughts that leave us with an emotional hangover are sourced from the nightmare. The vibration of our thoughts will either enlighten our body and mind, or they will deteriorate it. This is a spectrum and there are infinite degrees of vibrations - from the lowest low to the highest high.

We can only perceive of a certain spectrum of these vibrational frequencies. For instance, we cannot perceive of the lowest sound that an elephant makes or the squeal of a bat. But they exist. They are real. Remember that, just because we can't see, hear, taste or feel it, doesn't mean it isn't real. This is a very good point to meditate upon. If we can't hear sounds that we know exist, what else are we not perceiving? Awareness is bliss. Our divine essence is Awareness. So the state of delusion is the opposite of who we are. No wonder it is painful. Pain is the touchstone of something that needs to change.

While we are in the Gate of Delusion, we will likely not be open to reading this book at all. We have made up our mind that we are a victim, that the Universe has no order and makes no sense. We will feel misunderstood and unworthy. In recovery, this is called the "pity pot." I don't like saying that, but it is correct in this case.

A person in the Gates of Delusion is railing at the Universe. They are pitching a spiritual temper tantrum. People can get caught in this phase for a single day or for several lifetimes. Remember that the curriculum is not up to us; according to ACIM, it is only up to us when we partake in it. So let us not waste time.

It is highly suggested that we try to find others who can accompany we on our journey. At this point, it is also suggested to either start a group that has similar intentions and that uses these tools, or we can form our own Rainbow Gates group. We can visit the Rainbow Gates website for more information.

There are many Paths out of the Nightmare of Nowhere and our friends don't have to take the same Path. It is just important to find them in our new place. If we do not have someone to lean on for support, it might be a longer journey. On this Path we are most likely to meet "the One" who is a soul mate, partner of destiny or twin flame.

Sometimes it will seem as though we speak a totally different language than most. People might even say, "You're not from here, are you?" I have been asked that question more than once and they didn't mean 'from the South." We will also notice that we do not understand their language either. We relate less and less to worldly motivations. More likely, we will find that we are just not interested. Not to worry. This just indicates that our vibrational frequency is changing.

As our frequency rises, other people who have a lower frequency will fall away. We will just not click with them anymore. Twin flames and soul mates that are in relationship must be aware of this. Mine recently declared, "I became vegetarian because my wife did. I've got to keep up so we don't grow apart." He's a wise man.

As we awaken, we will also notice that gossip no longer carries the sizzle that it used to. Complaining about our situation now feels like we're lying because we know that we are in charge of our perception and our reality. Self-honesty will keep us moving forward. Overall, our life can be as miraculous and joyful as we desire it to be. However, we might be so used to living in the suffering of Nowhere that we do not require that much love, joy and abundance at this time. No worries, as love, joy and abundance become more familiar to us, their opposites fade. We are awakening from a bad dream. We will find that we become more and more aware of the love that surrounds us and *is* us. Love is who we are.

To work the Rainbow Gates, use the *Rainbow Gates* workbook. It might be most compatible in terminology. If we have come from a background in recovery, we will already be familiar with some of the workbooks that relate to particular recovery programs. Again, it is useful to have spiritual advisors, therapists or friends who will also work the Rainbow Gates along with us.

We are here at the best time in the history of the world. We can now find almost any information that pertains to spiritual enlightenment. Here are some subjects that gave me answers on my journey:

- quantum physics
- A Course In Miracles
- Laws of Attraction
- visualization
- affirmations
- meditation
- vibrational frequency clearing
- Emotional Freedom Technique (tapping)
- neuro-linguistics
- string theory
- "The Secret"
- "What the Bleep do We Know"
- Reiki
- binaural beats
- Native American ceremony
- Christianity
- East Indian philosophies
- Channeling
- 12 Steps of AA and NA

This is but a short list of topics that may be explored. Each topic provides further understanding of the various universes. (Yes, I said universes.)

The choice is ours as to how long we visit the Nightmare of Nowhere. Like any traveler, if we stay too long, we might get mired in the culture or find that our passport gets lost. Then we become a resident. The contrast that we experience is a learning tool in itself. We do not berate our self. Just learn from that contrast, and then pick up our tools.

Take a nap, meditate, read affirmations, write a gratitude list, get a massage, read inspirational material, make amends. Making amends can also be a powerful part of getting Somewhere. If we become stuck in Nowhere, just remember that we cannot do something to others without doing it to our self first. Our mind knows no difference. So we act loving to our self and make amends to others promptly (which is essentially the same thing). Amends is love and love is amends. Amends is just one expression of love. As we progress, we will see the nightmare shift back to the happy dream, right before our eyes. Don't block it by watching the details. Just let it happen. "Let go and let God."

If we ever get stuck in the Nightmare of Nowhere again, we have what we need to secure our release. But consider that, at times, we might be there for a reason.

Not only are we learning some valuable lesson, but our True Power can use us to help others. As is mentioned in the 6th and 7th Gates, this could be the reason that certain character traits have not been lifted from us. Our True Power might have needed us to retain some of the language and the culture so that we can be a "way shower" for those who are still living in our part of Nowhere. If so, show them compassion. The point is that nothing goes to waste in God's economy.

Some people desperately want to awaken from the Nightmare of Nowhere, but there are many people who do not even realize that they are there. We do not argue with them about their location. They do not believe us anyway. So we get on our merry way, back across the rainbow to our happy dream.

But for those who quietly whisper to us, "Do you know the way out?" We will share with them, "This is a way that I know. But you must be brave because it's Somewhere over the Rainbow."

Appendix: 12 Rainbow Gates

1. *We admitted we felt powerless. We ceased fighting.*
2. *We came to believe that cooperation with our True Power and Universal Laws would restore us to sanity.*
3. *We made a decision to cooperate with our True Power and consciously utilize the Universal Laws*
4. *We made a courageous and thorough personal and gratitude inventory.*
5. *We admitted to our self, True Power and another human being the exact nature of our blocks to the awareness of love.*
6. *We became ready to have these blocks to the awareness of love removed.*
7. *We sincerely asked our True Power to remove the blocks to the awareness of love, seeing our self as our True Power sees us.*
8. *We made a list of all persons, including our self, that we acted unloving toward and became willing to make amends with them all.*
9. *We made direct amends to such people wherever possible and when helpful.*
10. *We continued to take a daily gratitude and personal inventory and when we were unloving promptly admitted it.*
11. *We sought through prayer and meditation to improve our conscious contact with our True Power, praying only for knowledge of its will for us and the power to carry that out.*
12. *Having had a spiritual awakening we continued to practice these principles in all our affairs.*

Appendix: The 12 Steps of AA [41]

1. We admitted we were powerless over alcohol—that our lives had become unmanageable.
2. Came to believe that a Power greater than ourselves could restore us to sanity.
3. Made a decision to turn our will and our lives over to the care of God *as we understood Him.*
4. Made a searching and fearless moral inventory of ourselves.
5. Admitted to God, to ourselves, and to another human being the exact nature of our wrongs.
6. Were entirely ready to have God remove all these defects of character.
7. Humbly asked Him to remove our shortcomings.
8. Made a list of all persons we had harmed, and became willing to make amends to them all.
9. Made direct amends to such people wherever possible, except when to do so would injure them or others.
10. Continued to take personal inventory and when we were wrong promptly admitted it.
11. Sought through prayer and meditation to improve our conscious contact with God, *as we understood Him,* praying only for knowledge of His will for us and the power to carry that out.
12. Having had a spiritual awakening as the result of these Steps, we tried to carry this message to alcoholics, and to practice these principles in all our affairs.

---

[41] (Alcoholics Anonymous asked the author to print Steps after Gates)

The Twelve Steps of Alcoholics Anonymous are reprinted and adapted with permission of Alcoholics Anonymous World Services, Inc. ("AAWS") Permission to adapt the Twelve Steps does not mean that AAWS has reviewed or approved the contents of this publication, or that AAWS necessarily agrees with the views expressed herein. A.A. is a program of recovery from alcoholism only - use of the Twelve Steps in connection with programs and activities which are patterned after A.A., but which address other problems, or in any other non-A.A. context, does not imply otherwise.

Appendix: Quotes and Slogans

- Don't quit before the miracle happens.
- Easy does it but do it.
- Having resentment is like taking poison and expecting the other person to die.
- This too shall pass.
- First Things First
- Don't sweat the small stuff...It's all small stuff.
- You can't save your face and you're a** at the same time.
- Our goal is progress not perfection.
- G.O.D.- good orderly direction
- G.U.S. – Great Universal Spirit
- I can't. We can. Let's do this!
- More will be revealed.
- K.I.S.S. - Keep it simple silly!
- Grow or go!
- If you find yourself eating pooh sandwich, chances are that you ordered it!
- If nothing changes, then nothing changes!
- If you spot it, you got it.
- Pain is the touchstone of growth; suffering is optional.
- It's not the tree that trips you up- it's the roots.

- Happiness is not necessarily getting what you want- it's appreciating what you have,.
- There are no strangers here, only friends we haven't met.
- The greatest gift we have is the present.
- If you feel like you don't belong then be of service.
- There's safety in numbers. One through twelve.
- Wisdom is knowledge you learn after you know it all.
- The more I learn the less I realize I know.
- We are called to unity, not uniformity.
- You don't have to wait till the basement to get off the down elevator
- The joy is in the journey!
- I gave up everything for one thing, now I've given up that one thing and received everything.
- I can do something for 24 hours that would appall me if I had to keep it up for a lifetime.
- When my insides match my outside, I'm practicing a good program.
- Everything that irritates us about others can lead us to an understanding of our self.
- The 12 Rainbow Gates are a school in which we are all learners and all teachers.
- Let go and let God.

- Let go or be dragged! – Tara Meadows
- Be nice to newcomers ...one day they may be your spiritual advisor.
- The Rainbow Gates are education without graduation.
- In order to change we must be sick and tired of being sick and tired.
- The flip side to resentments is forgiveness.
- Trust God.........clean house........help others.
- Let a joy keep you. Reach out your hands and take it when it runs by.
- Peace or bust! – MA LAXMI ANAND
- What I am looking for is not out there. It is in me.
- Your True Power doesn't consult your past to determine your future.
- Replaying the past over and over again will ruin your present. Let it go. A brand new future awaits you.
- First things first.
- Never look down on anyone unless you are helping them up.
- I lose when I compare my insides with their outsides.

- Your True Power doesn't always give you what you ask for not because you don't deserve it, but because you deserve better!

- Sometimes you are delayed where you are because the Universe knows there is a storm where you're headed. Be grateful.

- Remember nothing is going to happen today that you and your True Power can't handle.

- Live life today as though you knew you were dying.

- Trust is lost in buckets and gained back in drops.

- You have to change you're playthings, playmates, and playgrounds to change your future.

- If I have one eye on yesterday and one eye on tomorrow, I'll be cockeyed today!

- Awakening is not something you get; it's something you work for.

- The first thing you put ahead of your awakening will be the second thing you lose.

- Attitude is the difference between an ordeal and an adventure!

- The slogans are Band-aids; the Gates are the cure; your True Power is the doctor.

- In my nightmares I was running from the dark. Now that I am awakening I am walking toward the light. – LS
- By changing attitudes and finding solutions, we can regain our sense of hope, serenity, freedom, and joy.
- You are not guilty for having a Nightmare, but you are responsible for your Awakening.- MA LAXMI ANAND
- Every day is a day when we must carry the vision of our True Power's will into all our activities.
- Everyone eventually awakens.- MA LAXMI ANAND
- It's nice living in the solution instead of the pollution.
- Gratitude is the hinge upon which an Awakened life swings.- MA LAXMI ANAND
- When you dance with a gorilla it is the gorilla who decides when to stop.
- The 12 Rainbow Gates are impossible to pass through alone. But there can be many helping hands if we just pick up the phone.
- There is no physical solution to a spiritual problem. -LS
- Anger is but one letter away from danger.

- If you woke up breathing today, congratulations! You get another chance!
- Don't count the Days, Make the Days Count.
- Forgiveness is giving up hope for a better past.
- You don't have to forget to forgive. - MA LAXMI ANAND
- It's not old behavior if it's still happening.
- Faith without works is dead.
- We will intuitively know how to handle situations which used to baffle us.
- Forgiveness is the attribute of the strong.- Ghandi[42]
- Happiness is when what you think, what you say and what you do are in harmony. – Ghandi
- Be the change you wish to see in the world.- Ghandi
- First they ignore you, then they laugh at you, then they fight you, then you win. – Ghandi
- Strength does not come from physical capacity. It comes from indomitable will. – Ghandi
- Do the footwork and let go of the results.
- A person is but the products of his thoughts. What she thinks she becomes. – Ghandi
- An eye for an eye only ends up making the whole world blind. – Ghandi

[42] Following quotes retrieved from BrainyQuote.com. Retrieved August 13, 2014

- When I admire the wonders of a sunset or the beauty of the moon, my soul expands in the worship of the creator. – Ghandi
- Humanity is an ocean; if a few drops are dirty, the ocean does not become dirty. – Ghandi
- A good man is the friend of ALL living things. – Ghandi
- Anger and intolerance are the enemies of correct understanding. – Ghandi
- In a gentle way, you can shake the world. – Ghandi
- Nobody can hurt me without my permission. – Ghandi
- Action expresses priorities. – Ghandi
- You can chain me, you can torture me, you can even destroy this body, but you will never imprison my mind. – Ghandi
- My life is my message. – Ghandi
- The essence of all religions is one. Only their approaches are different. – Ghandi
- Always aim at complete harmony of thought, word and deed. Always aim at purifying your thoughts and everything will be well. – Ghandi
- We need to find God and he cannot be found in noise. – Mother Teresa
- Peace begins with a smile.- Mother Teresa

- Joy is a net of love by which we can catch souls.
  – Mother Teresa
- We shall never know all the good a simple smile can do. – Mother Teresa
- Insanity is repeating the same mistake expecting different results- Einstein
- Weakness of attitude becomes weakness of character.   –Einstein
- The only reason for time is so that everything doesn't happen at once. – Einstein
- We cannot solve our problems with the same mind we used when we created them. – Einstein
- A person who never made a mistake never tried anything new. – Einstein
- When the solution is simple, God is answering. – Einstein
- Logic will get you from A to B. Imagination will take you everywhere. – Einstein
- A question that sometimes drives me crazy: am I or are the others crazy? – Einstein
- I have no special talent. I am only passionately curious. – Einstein
- There are two ways to live: you can live as if nothing is a miracle; you can live as if everything is a miracle.   –Einstein

- Have patience with all things, But, first of all with yourself.- St. Francis
- Never be in a hurry; do everything with a calm spirit.   – St. Francis
- Do not lose your inner peace for anything whatsoever, even if your whole world seems upset. – St. Francis
- Half an hour's meditation each day is essential, except when you are busy. Then a full hour is needed.   – St. Francis
- When you encounter difficulties and contradictions, do not try to break them, but bend them with gentleness and time. – St. Francis
- There was never an angry man who thought his anger unjust. – St. Francis
- Do not wish to be anything but what you are, and try to be that perfectly. – St. Francis
- To live according to the spirit is to love according to the spirit. – St. Francis
- Do not lose courage in considering your own imperfections. – St. Francis
- By turning your eyes on God in meditation, you whole soul will be filled with God. Begin all your prayers in the presence of God. – St. Francis.

- True progress quietly and persistently moves along without notice. – St. Francis
- Those who love to be feared fear to be loved. – St. Francis
- It is better to understand than to be understood. - St. Francis
- Faith is the first step even when you don't see the whole staircase. – Martin Luther King (MLK)
- The ultimate measure of a man is not where he stands in moments of comfort and convenience, but where he stands at times of challenge and controversy. – MLK
- Darkness cannot drive out darkness; only light can do that. Hate cannot drive out hate; only love can do that. - Martin Luther King
- There is nothing more dangerous than sincere ignorance and conscientious stupidity. – Martin Luther King
- He who is devoid of the power to forgive is devoid of the power to love. – Martin Luther King
- Our lives begin to end the day we become silent about things that matter. – Martin Luther King

Appendix: About the Author

MA LAXMI ANAND has been a spiritual seeker since the age of twelve. She overcame multiple addictions, and later, disabling depression after losing a 13 year court battle to have contact with her minor children. She rehabilitated herself in recovery gaining a Master's degree in the process. She's been a lighting technician, life guard, real estate agent, blues-singer, and taxi-cab driver.

MA LAXMI's marriage to the love of her life and a self-proclaimed "recovering sociopath" gave her the experience needed to realize the function and meaning of true partnership. She views true partnership as a path to quantum awakening.

Her business adventures demonstrate she understands mindful and miraculous business practices. Co-founding the nonprofit, ARG, was accomplished with pending bankruptcy, foreclosure and eviction while negotiating with a city hostile toward the housing rights of her clients.

MA LAXMI ANAND navigated the storm of discrimination and ended up securing their housing rights for several years in NC. Additionally, MA LAXMI is one of the first to crack the insurance code in her industry.

As a counselor, spiritual advisor or addiction specialist MA LAXMI guides outwardly successful people toward inner success by showing them how to harness their true power. It's a transformative power that changes people and the world around them. Some people describe MA LAXMI as inspiring, highly knowledgeable, illuminating but a bit of obsessive. If you would like to know more about MA LAXMI ANAND or the Rainbow Gates visit www.Facebook/12RainbowGates.com, where you can message MA LAXMI.

Or email 12RainbowGates@gmail.com

Appendix: A Word from Our Sponsor

Asheville Recovery Group (ARG) was a very unique agency which provides supportive services (housing, food, case management, drug screening, accountability, etc.) to adults having a diagnosed substance addiction that causes impairments impacting their ability to function independently within the community. Unfortunately, the community did not support it and it closed.

MA LAXMI ANAND now lives works in paradise like South Florida and support this work herself. She is certified in advanced yoga and Trauma Release Exercise (TRE) which goes very well with this work. You can check out information on Trauma Release Exercise on TraumaPrevention.org. Ma Laxmi is the first certified in Broward/Dade Florida and works out of Dania Beach.

Also there is now a companion workbook to "Realizing Emerald City", "The Complete Rainbow Gates Workbook: Quantum Healing for Emerging and Practicing Lightworkers." It can be found on Amazon.

Namaste